D1496156

ENCYCLOPEDIA OF ISLAMIC DOCTRINE

VOLUME 4
INTERCESSION
(*SHAFAA, TAWASSUL, ISTIGHATHA*)

SHAYKH MUHAMMAD HISHAM KABBANI

AS-SUNNA FOUNDATION OF AMERICA

As-Sunna Foundation of America
© 1998, 2nd edition, Shaykh Muhammad Hisham Kabbani

Edited by Gabriel F. Haddad, Ph.D. (Columbia), Alexandra
Bain, Ph.D. (Victoria), Karim K. Tourk, Jennifer McLennan

Library of Congress Cataloging in Publication Data

Kabbani, Shaykh Muhammad Hisham.
Encyclopedia of Islamic Doctrine Vol. 4. Intercession (*shafaa,
tawassul, istighatha*)
[Arabic title: *al-Musuat al-islami aqida ahl al-sunnah wa al-
jamaat*]
p.   cm.
    Indices.
Islam—doctrines. 2. Heretics, Muslim. 3. Wahhabiyah.
I. Kabbani, Shaykh Muhammad Hisham. II. Title.

ISBN: 1-871031-85-0

Published by
As-Sunna Foundation of America Publications
607A W. Dana St.
Mountain View, CA 94041
e-mail: asfa@sunnah.org
www: http://sunnah.org

Distributed by
KAZI Publications
3023 W. Belmont Avenue
Chicago, IL 60618
Tel: 773-267-7001; Fax: 773-267-7002
e-mail: kazibooks@kazi.org
www: http://www.kazi.org

CONTENTS

INTRODUCTION

This volume addresses the following questions:

What is the position of mainstream Islamic scholars on seeking means of approach to Allah (*tawassul*) through the Prophet (ﷺ) and the saints as in seeking their intercession (*shafaa*)?

How is the mainstream Islamic position contradicted by the "Salafi" claim that one of the "ten actions that negates Islam" is "relying on an intermediary between oneself and Allah when seeking intercession?"[1]

How is the mainstream Islamic position contradicted by Albani's claims that *tawassul* is not through the person of the Prophet (ﷺ) after his time, but through his supplication (*dua*) and only in his lifetime?

Why is it incorrect to associate seeking means of approach (*tawassul*) to Allah and asking for intercession through the Prophet (ﷺ) with the Christian worship (*ibada*) of Jesus as God, and of the saints? Is seeking means of approach to Allah through the Prophet (ﷺ) not entirely different from worshipping Allah?

What is the position of mainstream Islam on seeking blessings (*tabarruk*) through the Prophet's relics as opposed to that of those who say that seeking these blessings lies outside Islam?

What is the position of mainstream Islam on invoking blessings and peace (*salawat* and *salam*) on the Prophet (ﷺ)

1 Muhammad Saeed al-Qahtani, *al-Wala wa al-bara according to the doctrine of the Salaf*. al-Firdous Ltd: London, 1993.

as opposed to the position of those who impose limitations on it?

If they had only, when they were unjust to themselves,
come unto thee and asked Allah's forgiveness,
and the Messenger had asked forgiveness for them,
they would have found Allah indeed Oft-Returning,
Most Merciful (4:64)

Praise be to Allah, Lord of all the worlds, and blessings and peace of Allah upon His Prophet and Messenger, Muhammad, his Family, and all his Companions. There is not one single act of worship in Islam that is not performed as a means of approach to Allah (*tawassul*). Therefore it is inadmissible to say that seeking means of approach to Allah (*tawassul*) is not an integral and central part of Islam. It is the very heart of Islam, as even the bearing witness (*shahada*) expresses belief in seeking means of approach to Allah (*tawassul*), for one cannot be a Muslim unless one acknowledges the messengership and prophethood of Muhammad (ﷺ) and of all prophets. The goal of seeking means of approach to Allah (*tawassul*) remains Allah alone, Who said, *"I created the jinn and humankind only that they might worship Me"* (51:56). Therefore *tawassul* is seeking an obligatory means to an obligatory end. Similarly, the pillars of Islam each consist of actions that are a means to Allah for the one who performs them.

Intercession (*shafaa*) is the greatest means as only through intercession will the people of the fire enter paradise. Allah even called Himself 'Intercessor/Mediator' in the verse, *"You have not, beside Him, a protecting friend or mediator"* (32:4). Also, in a hadith narrated by Muslim, the Prophet (ﷺ) said:

> Allah will say, 'The angels have interceded. The prophets have interceded. The believers have interceded. There does not remain except the Most Merciful of the merciful ones.[2]

The Prophet (ﷺ) also called the Quran an intercessor, declared that people were intercessors, offering as example the

2 Narrated by Muslim (*iman*) from Abu Said al-Khudri.

intercession of children for the parents who lost them in their infancy. We ask for the intercession of the dead every time we pray the prescribed funeral prayer for the dead (*salat al-janaza*), when we say, "O Allah, do not prevent their benefit from reaching us (*allahumma la tahrimna ajrahum*)," Allah declares that the best people are the prophets, then the absolutely truthful (*siddiqin*)—and these are the great saints—then the martyrs (*shuhada*), and then the righteous (*salihin*). The Prophet (✺) declared that every person will be interceding on the Day of Resurrection, but in order of priority, as Allah gives precedence in this world to those who are closest to Him. This is a great blessing from Allah to the worlds and the reason why we are greatly blessed on this earth despite our sins. For the earth is never void of the true worshippers, and there is always someone left saying "Allah." Once this is realized, there will never be any doubts about Muslims availing themselves of the blessings and guidance that Allah sends to them in the persons of the the prophets (*anbiya*) and saints (*awliya*).

The friendship with Allah that is established in prophethood (*nubuwwa*) and sainthood (*wilaya*) does not stop with death. The claim that the Prophet (✺) is dead and gone having delivered his message is therefore strenuously rejected by mainstream Islam. He is alive and sustained by Allah (*hasha, wa taala Allahu amma yasifun*), our greetings reach him, our actions are seen by him, he intercedes for us, and the dust of his grave is the most blessed spot on earth, for which no show of love and honor is too great. No one who has love in their heart approaches the Prophet's grave without proper manners (*adab*). It is the responsibility of every Muslim to determine what is correct and what is wrong, and seeking means of approach to Allah (*tawassul*)—is first and foremost through the Prophet (✺). This is correct, recommended, and one of the greatest means of drawing close to Allah. Such has been the position of an overwhelming majority of scholars until our own time, opposed only by a handful of dissenters.

Tawassul is not restricted to the wealthy, and its validity is not determined by circumstance, analogy, or personal feelings,

but by solid, known legal proofs, and the practice of the righteous early generations. It is not a matter of procedure and
scholarship but one of sound belief. Disdain for asking the
Prophet's help demonstrates arrogance toward Allah's greatest
mercy, dislike for the Prophet (ﷺ), and a diseased heart. May
Allah protect us from such illness, especially in our era, which
is a time of fear of declaring love for our Prophet (ﷺ) and of
rampant disaffection towards him. As for seeking means of
approach to Allah (*tawassul*) with the saints, we say this: no
one can claim that they know Allah better than the Prophet
(ﷺ), just as no one can claim that they know the Prophet (ﷺ)
better than the Friends of Allah (saints, *awliya*). What then is
the status of one who would stop seeking their company and
asking for their help and guidance?

1. PROOF OF INTERCESSION (*SHAFAA*) IN ISLAMIC DOCTRINE

In Islam, the believer's every action is an intercession on his behalf. While he himself is the greatest intercessor other than Allah, the Prophet (ﷺ) has told us that the Quran also will intercede for us on the Day of Resurrection.[1] The Prophet's role as intercessor between creation and Creator is demonstrated by his position as the one whom Allah consults with regard to his Community. This is established by the following authentic hadith:[2]

> Hudhayfa said: "The Prophet (ﷺ) was absent and he did not come out until we thought that he would never come out again. When he did come out, he fell into such a long prostration that we thought that his soul had been taken back during that prostration. When he raised his head he said: 'My Lord sought my advice (*istasharani*) concerning my Community, saying, "What shall I do with them?" I said, "What You will, my Lord, they are Your creation and Your servants!" Then He sought my advice again (*fa istasharani al-thaniya*), and I said to Him the same thing, so He said, "We shall not put you to shame concerning your Community, O Muhammad."'
>
> Then He informed me that the first of my Community to enter paradise will be seventy thousand, each thousand of whom will have seventy thousand with them [four billion, nine hundred million], and none of them shall incur any accounting.
>
> Then He sent me a messenger who said, "Supplicate and it will be answered to you. Ask and it

---

1 Muslim, Ahmad, and others.
2 Narrated by Imam Ahmad in his *Musnad* (5:393), and Haythami said in *Majma al-zawaid* (10:68) that its chain was fair (*hasan*).

will be given to you." I said to His messenger, "Will my
Lord give me whatever I ask for?" He replied, "He did
not send me to you except to give you whatever you
ask for."

And indeed my Lord has given me whatever I
asked for, and I say this without pride: He has forgiv-
en me my sins past or future while I am still alive and
walking about, He has granted me that my
Community shall not starve, and shall not be over-
come. He has given me al-Kawthar, a river of paradise
which flows into my pond. He has given me power and
victory over my enemies, and terror running in their
ranks at a month's distance from my Community. He
has granted me that I be first among the prophets to
enter paradise. He has made spoils of war lawful and
good for me and my Community, and He has made
lawful much of what He had forbidden those before
us, nor did He take us to task for it.[3]

According to the Sharia (divine law), a good action by even
the greatest apostate intercedes for him and profits him. This
is established by Bukhari when he relates that because Abu
Lahab freed his slave Thuwayba on the day the Prophet (ﷺ)
was born, his punishment in the grave is diminished every
Monday. One major principle of the above hadith is that the
benefit of intercession takes place before resurrection. Scholars
have also quoted this hadith to highlight the importance of
praising the Prophet (ﷺ) and to emphasize that even non-
believers benefit from actions that denote his praise–however
unintentional. One such scholars is the *hafiz* of Syria and sup-
porter of Ibn Taymiyya, Muhammad ibn Abi Bakr al-Qaysi,
known as Nasir al-Din al-Dimashqi (A.H. 777-842), who has
written several books on the praiseworthiness of celebrating
Prophet Muhammad's (ﷺ) birthday (*mawlid*).

Some ask whether persons other than the Prophet (ﷺ) can
be intercessors as well. The answer is yes, since the Prophet
(ﷺ) has explicitly declared so in many sound hadith that are
quoted below, including the following:

3 Among them are *Jami al-athar fi mawlid al-nabi al-mukhtar* (The compendium
of reports concerning the birth of the chosen prophet), *al-Lafz al-raiq fi mawlid khayr
al-shalaiq* (The shining expressions for the brith of the best of creation) and *Mawrid
al-sadi bi mawlid al-nabi al-hadi* (The continuous spring: the birth of the guiding pro-
het) and the *hafiz* Shams al-Din al-Jazari in his book *Urf al-tarif bi al-mawlid al-sharif*
(The beneficient communication of the noble birth of the Prophet (ﷺ).

More people than the collective tribes of Banu
Tamim shall enter Paradise due to the intercession of
one man from my Community. It was asked, "O
Messenger of Allah, is it other than you?" He said,
"Other than me."[4]

The belief in the Prophet's intercession, and that of others,
is obligatory in Islam. This is stated clearly by Imam al-
Tahawi, Ghazali, al-Ashari, and even by Ibn Taymiyya.[5] The
intercession of the Prophet (ﷺ) and others is a mercy from
Allah and it is an obligation and an order for mankind to seek
out Allah's mercy.

The seeking of intercession has two effects: one is immedi-
ate, in increasing the faith of the person and offering him all
sorts of benefits in the world, and the other is delayed until the
resurrection.

The statement in *al-Wala wa al-bara,* which states that
among the "ten actions that negate Islam" is "relying on an
intermediary between oneself and Allah when seeking intercession,"[6] is completely rejected by mainstream Islam, since
according to the Holy Quran, even the Jews sought the
Prophet's intercession before his time:[7]

> *And when there came to them a (true) Book from
> Allah [the Quran] verifying that which they have [the
> Torah], and aforetime [before the Quran was revealed]
> they used to pray for victory against those who disbe-
> lieve [saying: O Allah, grant us victory against them
> by the intermediary and help of the Prophet that is to
> be sent at the end of time], but when there came to
> them [the Prophet; the truth which they knew from the
> Torah, namely, the advent of the Prophet] that which
> they did not recognize, they disbelieved in him [due to
> envy and aversion to their loss of authority]; so Allah's
> curse is on the unbelievers.*[8]

4 Narrated by Tirmidhi (*hasan sahih gharib*).

5 More specifically, in the *Aqida tahawiyya* of Imam al-Tahawi, in Ghazali's *al-
Iqtisad* and the chapter on *aqida* in his *Ihya,* in the works of al-Ashari, and in the
Aqida wasitiyya of Ibn Taymiyya.

6. Muhammad Saeed al-Qahtani, *al-Wala wa al-bara,* p.99.

7 As explained by Suyuti and al-Mahalli in *Tafsir al-jalalayn.*

8 Verse 2:89; Muhammad Shakir's translation togther with *Tafsir al-jalalayn.*

Concerning the above verse, Suyuti said:[9]

> Ibn Abi Hatim narrated through Said or Ikrima from Ibn Abbas: The Jews used to pray for the Prophet [Muhammad's (ﷺ)] victory against the Aws and Khazraj [tribes in Madina], before he was sent. Then, when Allah sent him from among the Arabs, they disbelieved in him. They denied and rejected what they used to say about him. At this Muadh ibn Jabal, Bishr ibn al-Bara, and Dawud ibn Salama: "O Jews! Fear Allah and submit! For you used to pray for victory against us through Muhammad when we were disbelievers, and you used to tell us that he is a Messenger soon to be sent, and you would describe him for us." Whereupon Salam ibn Mashkam, one of the Jewish tribe of Banu Nadir, said, "He did not come to us with something that we recognize, and he is not the one that we used to describe and speak about before." For this reason Allah revealed the verse.

This evidence shows that the statement in *al-Wala wa al-bara* whereby among the "ten actions that negate Islam" is "relying on an intermediary between oneself and Allah when seeking intercession" is deceptive and self-contradictory, since the meaning of intercession is to act as an intermediary. How can one at the same time seek an intermediary and refrain from relying on him? This would not be the act of a believer but of a duplicitous person. Language and logic aside, it is clear in the Hadith of Intercession in Bukhari and Muslim that the people will seek intercessors among all the prophets until they come to the Seal of Prophets seeking to rely upon him for intercession, and he confirms that he is able to fulfill their request. This is one of the matters that the Prophet (ﷺ) emphasized in the hadith "I have been given five things . . ." What then is the effect of dismissing reliance on an intercessor to an "action that negates Islam" other than to reduce the status of the Prophet (ﷺ) and his intercession?

Allah has created intercession as He has created everything else—out of mercy. He said, *"My Mercy encompasses all things"* (7:156). No doubt His greatest Mercy is the Prophet (ﷺ), about whom He said, *"We did not send you save as a Mercy to the worlds"* (21:107). Belief in the Prophet's intercession is tied to

9 Suyuti, *Asbab al-nuzul.*

the believers' bearing witness to the truth he brought and their recognition of his right as Allah's greatest Mercy. Although the angels also intercede according to Quran, the Prophet (࿇) is nearer to Allah than the nearest among them. No one will speak on the Day of Judgment except those who have permission, and it is related in authentic hadith that Allah gave such permission to the Prophet (࿇). The Prophet (࿇) will not be saying "I and Myself" but will be saying *ummati, ummati* "My Community." Such intercession cannot be expected or looked forward to, as the "Salafis" try to suggest.

Allah said in *Surah Yunus*:

> *Is it a matter of wonderment to men that We have sent Our revelation to a man from among themselves? That he should warn mankind and give the glad tidings to the believers that they have with their Lord a truthful foothold / forerunner. But the unbelievers say, 'This is an evident sorcerer'*(10:2).

The following is one of the authoritative explanations for the expression "a truthful foothold/forerunner" (*qadama sidqin*):

"A truthful foothold/forerunner" is mentioned in the following sources:

• Bukhari in his *Sahih*[10]
• Tabari in *Jami al-bayan*
• Qurtubi in *al-Jami li al-ahkam*
• Ibn Uyayna in his *Tafsir*
• Ibn Kathir in his *Tafsir*
• Suyuti in *al-Durr al-manthur* and *al-Riyad al-aniqa*
• Abu al-Fadl al-Maydani in *Majma al-amthal*
• Abu al-Shaykh (this is Abd Allah ibn Muhammad al-Asbahani)
• Ibn Mardawayh in his *Tafsir*
• Ibn Abi Hatim in his *Tafsir*

Others said, on the authority of the Companions Ali ibn Abi Talib, Abu Said al-Khudri, the *tabiin*, al-Hasan, Qatada,

---

10 Bukhari, Book of *tafsir* for *Surah Yunus*, ch. 1.

Mujahid, Zayd ibn Aslam, Bakkar ibn Malik, and Muqatil, "It is Muhammad, blessings and peace upon him."

Qurtubi said:

> It is Muhammad (ﷺ) for he is an intercessor whom the people obey and who precedes them, just as he said, I will be your scout at the Pond (*ana faratukum ala al-hawd*). And he was asked about its meaning and said, 'It is my intercession, for you to use me as a means to your Lord (*hiya shafaati tawassaluna bi ila rabbikum*)'.[11]

Al-Hakim al-Tirmidhi said, "Allah gave him precedence (*qaddamahu*) with the praiseworthy station (*al-maqam al-mahmud*). Qurtubi mentioned it.

Suyuti said:

> Ibn Jarir al-Tabari and Abu al-Shaykh narrated that al-Hasan said: It is Muhammad (ﷺ) who is an intercessor for them on the Day of Rising. Ibn Mardawayh narrated from Ali ibn Abi Talib through al-Harith and from Abu Said al-Khudri through Atiyya: It is Muhammad (ﷺ). He is an intercessor in truth on their behalf on the Day of Rising.

Intercession in no way diminishes the fact that everything is under Allah's sovereignty. It is Allah who created secondary causes and means, and He has said, "*Seek the ways to Allah*" (5:35). Intercession is but one of those means.

The intercession of the Prophet (ﷺ) is a thing to be greatly prized. While the utterance of the bearing witness to the oneness of Allah and the messengership of the Prophet (ﷺ) (*kalima*) incurs for the person who says it, the immense benefits of being Muslim, the Prophet's intercession is an additional benefit of saying, "There is no god but Allah (*la ilaha illa Allah*)." In fact, his intercession is guaranteed once the *kalima* is pronounced, thus ensuring that his intercession is to be prized at least as greatly as the passport to Islam.

Sincere love of the Prophet (ﷺ) and of pious people is a tremendous benefit, as one hopes thereby to be loved back. The

---

11 Ibn Kathir mentioned the latter meaning in his *Tafsir* (2:4-6. 4:183) as well as al-Razi in his (8:242).

Prophet (ﷺ) said to the Arab who had prepared nothing for the Final Hour other than love for Allah and His Prophet (ﷺ), "One is raised in the company of those he loves (*yuhshar al-mar ma man ahabb*)," and the Companions who were present said that hearing this promise was the happiest day of their lives.[12] All this implies reliance on an intercessor and contradicts the assertion of the book, *al-Wala wal-bara*, that "relying on an intermediary between oneself and Allah when seeking intercession negates Islam."

The asking of intercession from the intercessor, as the asking of prayer (*dua*) from a pious Muslim, in no way implies that the person who asks believes any good can come apart from Allah. In effect he is asking Allah, but he is using the means that Allah put at his disposal, including the intercession of those who may be closer than himself to Allah. To refuse to believe that any other may be closer than us to Allah is the sin of Iblis (Satan).

Imam Ghazali said in the section on doctrine of his *Ihya*:

> It is obligatory to believe in the intercession of first the prophets, then religious scholars, then martyrs, then other believers, the intercession of each one commensurate with his rank and position with Allah Most High.[13]

1.1. THE MEANING OF INTERCESSION

A contemporary scholar wrote the following explanation of the meaning of intercession:[14]

Intercession (*al-shafaa*) is derived in Arabic from *al-shaaf* which means "even" as opposed to odd, since the interceder adds his own recommendation to the plea of the petitioner; in this way the number of pleaders becomes even, and the weak plea of the petitioner is strengthened by the prestige of the intercessor. We are accustomed in our social and communal life to seek others' intercession and help for fulfilling our needs.

We resort to intercession to get an advantage or to ward off a disadvantage. Here we are not talking about an advantage or a disadvantage, a benefit or a harm that is caused by natural

---

12 Narrated in Bukhari.

13 Al-Ghazali, *Ihya ulum al-din* (beginning), trans. Nuh Keller in *Reliance of the Traveller* p. 824.

14 Al-Tabatabai, *al-Mizan: An Exegesis of the Quran*, 3rd ed. Surah 2, verses 47-48, vol. 1, pp. 221-262.

causes, like hunger and thirst, heat or cold, illness or health, because in such cases we get what we want through natural remedies, like eating and drinking, wearing clothes, getting treatment and so on. What we are talking here about is the benefit and harm, punishment and reward resulting from the social laws made by civil authorities.

From the nature of the relationship of mastership-and-servitude and, for that matter, between every ruler and ruled, rise some commandments, orders and prohibitions. One who follows and obeys them is praised and rewarded, and the one who disobeys is condemned and punished. That reward or punishment may be either material or spiritual. When a master orders his servant to do or not to do a thing, and the servant obeys him, he gets its reward; if he disobeys he is punished. Whenever a rule is made, the punishment for its infringement is laid down too. This is the foundation upon which all authorities are built.

When a man wants to get a material or spiritual benefit but is not suitably qualified for it, or when he desires to ward off a harm which is coming to him because of his disobedience, but has no shield to protect himself, then comes the time for intercession.

In other words, when he wants to get a reward without doing his task, or to save himself from punishment without performing his duty, then he looks for someone to intercede on his behalf. But intercession is effective only if the person for whom one intercedes is otherwise qualified to get the reward and has already established a relationship with the authority. If an ignorant person desires appointment to a prestigious academic post, no intercession can do him any good; nor can it avail in case of a rebellious traitor who shows no remorse for his misdeeds and does not submit to the lawful authorities. It clearly shows that intercession works as a supplement to the cause; it is not an independent cause.

The effect of an intercessor's words depends on one or the other factor which may have some influence upon the concerned authority. In other words, intercession must have a solid ground to stand upon.

The intercessor endeavors to find a way to the heart of the authority concerned, in order that the authority may give the reward to, or waive the punishment of, the person who is the subject of intercession. An intercessor does not ask the master to nullify his mastership or to release the servant from his servitude; nor does he plead with him to refrain from laying down rules and regulations for his servants or to abrogate his commandments (either generally or especially in that one case) in order to save the wrong-doer from the due consequences; nor does he ask him to discard the canon of reward and punishment (either generally or in that particular case).

In short, intercession can interfere with neither the institution of mastership and servantship nor the master's authority to lay down the rules; nor can it effect the system of reward and punishment. These three factors are beyond the jurisdiction of intercession.

What an intercessor does is this: he accepts the inviolability of the above mentioned three aspects. Then he looks at one or more of the following factors and builds his intercession on that basis:

* He appeals to such attributes of the master as give rise to forgiveness, e.g., his nobility, magnanimity and generosity.
* He draws attention to such characteristics of the servant as justify mercy and pardon, e.g., his wretchedness, poverty, low status and misery.
* He puts at stake his own prestige and honour in the eyes of the master.

Thus, the import of intercession is like this: I cannot and do not say that You should forget Your mastership over Your servant or abrogate Your commandment or nullify the system of reward and punishment. What I ask of You is to forgive this defaulting servant of Yours because You are magnanimous and generous, and because no harm would come to You if you forgive his sins; and/or because Your servant is a wretched creature of low status and steeped in misery, and it is befitting for a master like you to ignore the faults of a slave like him; and/or because You have bestowed on me a high prestige, and I implore You to forgive and pardon him in honor of my intercession.

The intercessor, in this way, bestows precedence on the factors of forgiveness and pardon over those of legislation and recompense. He removes the case from the latter's jurisdiction putting it under the former's influence. As a result of this shift, the consequences of legislation (reward and punishment) do not remain applicable. The effect of intercession is, therefore, based on shifting the case from the jurisdiction of reward and punishment to that of pardon and forgiveness; it is not a confrontation between one cause (divine legislation) and the other (intercession).

By now it should be clear that intercession is one of the causes; it is the intermediate cause that connects a distant cause to its desired effect. Allah is the Ultimate Cause. This causality shows itself in two ways:

• First, in creation: every cause begins with Him and ends with Him; He is the first and the final Cause. He is the real Creator and Originator. All other causes are mere channels to carry His boundless mercy and limitless bounty to His creatures.
• Second, in legislation: He, in His mercy, established contact with His creatures; He laid down the religion, sent down His commandments, and prescribed suitable reward and appropriate punishment for His obedient and disobedient servants. He sent prophets and apostles to bring us good tidings and to warn us of the consequences of transgression. The prophets and apostles conveyed to us His message in the best possible way. Thus, His proof over us was complete: *"And the word of your Lord has been accomplished with truth and justice, there is none to change His words"* (6:115).

Both aspects of causality of Allah may be, and in fact are, related to intercession:

1.1.1. INTERCESSION IN CREATION
Quite obviously the intermediary causes of creation are the

conduits that bring the Divine mercy, life, sustenance and other bounties to the creatures; and as such they are intercessors between the Creator and the created. Some Quranic verses are based on this very theme: *"Whatever is in the heavens and whatever is in the earth is His; who is he that can intercede with Him but by His permission"* (2:255); *"Surely your Lord is Allah, who created the heavens and the earth in six periods, and He is firmly established on the throne, regulating the affair; there is no intercessor except after His permission"* (10:3).

Intercession in the sphere of creation is only the intermediation of causes and effect between the Creator and the created thing, bringing it into being and regulating its affairs.

1.1.2. INTERCESSION IN LEGISLATION

Intercession, as analyzed earlier, is effective in this sphere too. It is in this context that Allah says, *"On that day shall no intercession avail except of him whom the Beneficent Allah allows and whose word He is pleased with"* (20:109); *"And intercession will not avail aught with Him save of him whom He permits"* (34:23); *"And how many an angel is there in the heavens whose intercession does not avail at all except after Allah has given permission to whom He pleases and chooses"* (53:26); *". . . and they do not intercede except for him whom He approves . . ."* (21:28); *"And those whom they call upon besides Him have no authority for intercession, but he who bears witness of the truth and they know (him)"* (43:86).

These verses clearly affirm an intercessory role for various servants of Allah, both human and angelic, with divine permission and pleasure. It means that Allah has given them some power and authority in this matter, and to Him belongs all the kingdom and all the affairs. Those intercessors may appeal to Allah's mercy, forgiveness and other relevant attributes to cover and protect a servant who otherwise would have deserved punishment because of his sins and transgressions. That intercession would transfer his case from the general law of recompense to the special domain of grace and mercy (it has already been explained that the effect of intercession is based on shifting a case from the former's to the latter's jurisdiction;

it is not a confrontation between one law and the other). Allah clearly says, ". . . *so these are they of whom Allah changes the evil deeds to good ones*" (25:70).

Allah has the power to change one type of deed into another, in the same way as He may render an act null and void. He says, "*And We will proceed to what they have done of deeds, so We shall render them as scattered floating dust*" (25:23); . . . "*so He rendered their deeds null*" (47:9); "*If you avoid the great sins which you are forbidden, We will expiate from you your sins*" (4:31); "*Surely Allah does not forgive that any thing should be associated with Him, and forgives what is besides that to whomsoever He pleases*" (4:48). The last quoted verse is certainly about the cases other than true belief and repentance, because with belief and repentance even polytheism is forgiven, like any other sin. Also Allah may nurture a small deed to make it greater than the original: "*These shall be granted their reward twice*" (28:54); "*Whoever brings a good deed, he shall have ten like it*" (6:160).

Likewise, He may treat a nonexistent deed as existing: "*And (as for) those who believe and their offspring follow them in faith, We will unite with them their offspring and We will not diminish to them aught of their work; every man is responsible for what he has done*" (52:21).

Allah does what He pleases, and decrees as He wills. Of course, He does so pursuant to His servants' interest, and in accordance with an intermediary cause, and intercession of the intercessors (e.g., the prophets, the saints and those who are nearer to Him) is one of those causes, and certainly no rashness or injustice is entailed therein. It should have been clear by now that intercession, in its true sense, belongs to Allah only; all His attributes are intermediaries between Him and His creatures and are the channels through which His grace, mercy and decrees pass to the creatures; He is the Real and All-Encompassing Intercessor: "*Say: Allah's is the intercession altogether*" (39:44); . . . "*you have not besides Him any guardian or any intercessor*" (32:4); . . . "*there is no guardian for them nor any intercessor besides Him*" (6:51). Intercessors other than

Allah only get that right by His permission, and by His authority. In short, intercession with Him is a confirmed reality in all cases where it does not go against the divine glory and honor.

1.2. PROOF-TEXTS OF INTERCESSION IN THE QURAN AND HADITH

1.2.1. LINGUISTIC DEFINITIONS

Shafaa is the Arabic noun for intercession or mediation or asking forgiveness from Allah for someone else. The word is used also in laying a petition before a king,[15] interceding for a debtor,[16] and in judicial procedure:

> *Whoso makes a righteous intercession shall partake of the good that ensues therefrom, and whoso makes an evil intercession will bear the consequence thereof* (4:85).

> He who by his intercession invalidates one of Allah's *hudud* (laws concerning transgressions) is challenging (*tahadda*) Allah.[17]

He who intercedes is called *shafi* and *shafa*.

1.2.2. THE ISLAMIC DOCTRINE OF INTERCESSION AND BELIEF THEREIN

Hujjat al-Islam Imam Ghazali said:

> It is obligatory to believe in the intercession of first the prophets, then religious scholars, then martyrs, then other believers, the intercession of each one commensurate with his rank and position with Allah Most High.[18]

Any believer remaining in hell without intercessor shall be

---

15 See *Lisan al-arab* under *shafaa*.
16 See Bukhari, *Istiqrad* ch. 18.
17 Bukhari, *Anbiya* ch. 54.
18 Cf. *"Allah Himself is witness that there is no god save Him. And the angels and the men of learning too bear witness"* (3:18) and *"Whoso obey Allah and the Messenger, they are with those unto whom Allah has shown favor, of the prophet and the saints and the martyrs and the righteous. The best of company are they!"* (4:69).

taken out of it by the favor of Allah, no one who believes remaining in it forever, and anyone with an atom's weight of faith in his heart will eventually depart from it.[19]

1.3. PROOF OF INTERCESSION AND MEDIATION IN THE QURAN

In the Holy Quran intercession is:

1 Negated in relation to the unbelievers
2 Established categorically as belonging to Allah
3 Further defined as generally permitted for others than Allah by His permission
4 Further specified as permitted for the angels on behalf of whomever Allah wills
5 Explicitly attributed to the Prophet (ﷺ) in his lifetime
6 Alluded to in reference to the Prophet (ﷺ) in the afterlife
7 Alluded to in reference to the generality of the prophets and the believers in the afterlife

1.3.1. THE DAY OF JUDGMENT

The Day of Judgment is described as a day on which no intercession will be accepted from the Children of Israel (2:48) or the unbelievers, generally speaking (2:254), or the idolaters (10:18, 74:48):

> And guard yourselves against a day when no soul will avail another, nor intercession be accepted from it (2:48).

> O believers, spend of that wherewith We have provided you before a day comes when there will be no trafficking, nor friendship, nor intercession. The disbelievers, they are the wrong-doers (2:254).

> They worship beside Allah that which neither hurts nor profits them, and they say: These are our intercessors with Allah (10:18).

> The mediation of mediators will not avail them then (74:48).

19 Al-Ghazzali, *Ihya ulum al-din* (beginning), trans. Nuh Keller in *Reliance of the Traveller* p. 824.

1.3.2. IN ABSOLUTE TERMS, INTERCESSION BELONGS TO ALLAH ALONE

Or choose they intercessors other than Allah? Say, What! Even though they have power over nothing and have no intelligence? Say, the intercession belongs to Allah (39:43-44).

1.3.3. INTERCESSION PERMITTED BY OTHERS BUT ONLY WITH HIS PERMISSION

A further definition that "intercession belongs to Allah" is that intercession is actually permitted to others than Allah, but only by His permission:

Who should intercede with Him, except by His permission? (2:255).

There is no intercessor save after His permission (10:3).

They will have no power of intercession, save him who has made a covenant with his Lord (19:87).

And those unto whom they cry instead of Him possess no power of intercession, except him who beareth witness unto the truth knowingly (43:86).

1.3.4. ANGELS PERMITTED TO INTERCEDE

Angels are permitted to intercede for whomever Allah wills, specifically among the believers:

And they say, the Beneficent hath taken unto Himself a son . . . Nay, but honored slaves [angels] . . . and they cannot intercede except for him whom He accepteth, and they quake for awe of Him (21:26-28).

Those who bear the Throne, and all who are round about it . . . ask forgiveness for those who believe (40:7).

The angels hymn the praise of their Lord and ask forgiveness for those on the earth (42:5).

1.3.5. THE INTERCESSION OF THE PROPHET (ﷺ) IN HIS LIFETIME IS EXPLICITLY AND FREQUENTLY ESTABLISHED

The intercession of the Prophet (ﷺ) in his lifetime is explicitly and frequently established in the Quran:

Pardon them and ask forgiveness for them and consult with them upon the conduct of affairs (3:159).

And if, when they had wronged themselves, they had but come unto thee and asked forgiveness of Allah, and the Messenger had asked forgiveness for them, they would have found Allah Forgiving, Merciful (4:64).

And ask forgiveness of Allah (for others). Allah is ever Forgiving, Merciful. And plead not on behalf of those who deceive themselves (4:106-107).

But Allah would not punish them while thou wast with them, nor will He punish them while they seek forgiveness (8:33).

Ask forgiveness for them (the hypocrites) or ask not forgiveness for them; though thou ask forgiveness for them seventy times Allah will not forgive them . . . And never pray for one of them who dieth, nor stand by his grave (9:80, 84).

Pray for them. Lo! thy prayer is an assuagement for them (9:103).

It is not for the Prophet, and those who believe, to pray for the forgiveness of idolaters even though they may be near of kin (to them) after it hath become clear that they are people of hell-fire (9:113).

If they ask thy leave for some affair of theirs, give leave to whom thou wilt of them, and ask for them forgiveness of Allah (24:62).

Know that there is no god save Allah, and ask forgiveness for thy sin and for believing men and believing women (47:19).

Accept their [believing women's] allegiance and ask Allah to forgive them (60:12).

And when it is said unto them, Come! The Messenger of Allah will ask forgiveness for you! They [the hypocrites] avert their faces and thou seest them turning away, disdainful. Whether thou ask forgiveness for them or ask not forgiveness for them, Allah will not forgive them (63:5-6).

1.3.6. INTERCESSION AND MEDIATION OF THE PROPHET (ﷺ) ON THE DAY OF JUDGMENT

The intercession and mediation of the Prophet (ﷺ) on the Day of Judgment has been established by the consensus of scholars (*ijma*) and is an article of belief in Islam as previously stated. The Mutazili heresy rejected it, as they held that the person who enters the fire will remain there forever. The consensus of scholars is based on the principle of permission (see the verses in section 1.3.3. above), on the allusive verses in the present section, and on the more explicit hadiths quoted further below:

It may be that thy Lord will raise thee to a praised station (17:79).

And verily thy Lord will give unto thee so that thou wilt be content (93:5).

1.3.7. INTERCESSION OF THE PROPHETS IN GENERAL

The intercession of the generality of the prophets as well as the believers has similarly been established by the verses of sections 1.3.3. and 1.3.5. above, i.e. based on permission, and also on that prophets have made a covenant with their Lord (33:7, 3:81) and do bear witness unto the truth knowingly. The latter is true also of the elite of the believers (3:18: Allah, the angels, and the men of learning). There are also the following verses concerning the prophets' intercession in their lifetime:

> And they said, O our father! Ask forgiveness of our
> sins for us for lo! we were sinful. And he [Jacob] said,
> I shall ask forgiveness for you of my Lord. He is the
> Forgiving, the Merciful (12:97-98).

> He [Abraham] said, 'Peace unto thee. I shall ask
> forgiveness of my Lord for thee' (19:47).

> Abraham promised his father, 'I will ask forgive-
> ness for thee, though I owe nothing for thee from Allah'
> (60:4).

There are also the following verses concerning the believers'
intercession in their lifetime:

> It is not for the Prophet, and those who believe, to
> pray for the forgiveness of idolaters even though they
> may be near of kin (to them) after it has become clear
> that they are people of hellfire (9:113).

> And those who came after them say, Our Lord!
> Forgive us and forgive our believing brothers who
> lived before us (59:10).

1.4. PROOF OF INTERCESSION AND MEDIATION IN THE HADITH

In the hadith, the power of intercession is emphasized as
having been given to:

- The Prophet (ﷺ) exclusively of other prophets
- Special members of the Prophet's Community, such as
saints and scholars
- The common believers of the Prophet's Community

1.4.1. INTERCESSION OF THE PROPHET (ﷺ)
1.4.1.1. IN HIS LIFETIME FOR THOSE WHO PASSED AWAY

- Muslim (janaiz): Abu Hurayra narrates that a dark-complexioned woman or young man used to sweep the mosque. When that person died, no-one told the Prophet (ﷺ) until he inquired about it and then went to pray over the grave. He remarked, "Verily, these graves are full of darkness for their dwellers. Verily, Allah Mighty and Glorious illumines them for their occupants by reason of my prayer for them."

• Muslim (janaiz): Awf ibn Malik said that after he heard the words of the Prophet's prayer over a dead person, he earnestly desired that he were that dead person.

• Muslim (janaiz): Muhammad ibn Qays narrates from Aisha that the Prophet (ﷺ) on every night that he was with her used to quietly get dressed and leave at the end of the night, and she once followed him surreptitiously until he reached Baqi [the graveyard of the believers] where he prayed for the dead. Later he told her that Gabriel had come to him and said, "Your Lord has commanded you to go to the inhabitants of Baqi and beg forgiveness for them."

This issue is also treated in the authentic traditions concerning the Prophet's prayer and *takbir* over the graves of the believers.

1.4.1.2. IN THE AFTERLIFE

• Al-Daraqutni, al-Dulabi, al-Bayhaqi, Khatib al-Baghdadi, al-Uqayli, Ibn Adi, Tabarani, and Ibn Khuzayma in his *Sahih*, all through various chains going back to Musa ibn Hilal al-Abdi from Ubayd Allah Ibn Umar, both from Nafi, from Ibn Umar: "Whoever visits my grave, my intercession will be guaranteed for him."

Ibn Hajar al-Haytami said in his commentary on Nawawi's *Idah fi manasik al-hajj*:

> Ibn Khuzayma narrated it in his *Sahih* but alluded to its weakness. Ibn al-Kharrat and Taqi al-Subki declared it sound (*sahih*). Daraqutni and Tabarani also narrate it with the wording: "Whoever visits me with no other need than visiting me, it is my duty to be his intercessor on the Day of Judgment." One version has: "It is Allah's duty that I be his intercessor on the Day of Judgment." Ibn al-Subki declared it sound.

Although declaring all the chains of this hadith imperfect (*layyina*), Dhahabi nevertheless said that they strengthened each other and declared the chain *jayyid* (good); that is, the hadith is *hasan*.[20] Sakhawi confirmed him in the *Maqasid al-hasana*, while al-Subki declared it *sahih* in *Shifa al-siqam*,[21] as did Samhudi in *Saadat al-darayn*.[22] Imam Lucknawi said, "And this [i.e. declaring it authentic] until today is the practice of the people who have attained mastery of this science."[23]

Dhahabi said about Musa ibn Hilal, "He is good enough in his narrations (*huwa salih al-hadith*)."[24] Ibn Adi said, "He (Musa ibn Hilal) is most likely acceptable; other people have called him unknown (*majhul*) and this is not true. He is one of the shaykhs of Imam Ahmad and most of them are trustworthy."[25] Lucknawi said, "Abu Hatim [al-Razi]'s saying whereby Musa ibn Hilal is unknown is rejected, because it is established that those who are trustworthy narrated hadith from him."[26]

Even Albani declared him *thabit al-riwaya* (of established reliability) in his *Irwa* (4:338).

Dhahabi calls Ubayd Allah ibn Umar al-Umari, "Truthful, of fair narrations (*saduq hasan al-hadith*).[27] Sakhawi says of him, "His narrations are good enough (*salih al-hadith*).[28] Ibn Main said to Darimi about him, "Good enough and trustworthy (*salih thiqa*)."[29]

Al-Lucknawi also said about this hadith in his book, "There are some who declared it weak, and others who asserted that all the hadiths on visitation of the Prophet (ﷺ) are forged, such as Ibn Taymiyya and his followers, but both positions are false for those who were given right understanding, for verification of the case dictates that the hadith is *hasan*, as Taqi al-Din al-Subki has expounded in his book *Shifa al-siqam fi ziyarat khayr al-anam*."[30]

---

20 Dhahabi, *Mizan al-itidal* (4:226).
21 Al-Subki, *Shifa al-siqam* p.12-13.
22 Samhudi, *Saadat al-darayn* 1:77.
23 Lucknawi, *al-Ajwiba al-fadily* p. 155.
24 Dhahabi, *Mizan* (3:220).
25 Ibn Adi, *al-Kamil fi al-duafa* (6:2350).
26 Lucknawi, *al-Raf wal-takmil* p. 248-249.
27 Dhahabi, *al-Mughni* (1:348).
28 Sakhawi, *al-Tuhfa al-latifa* (3:366).
29 Ibn Main, *al-Kamil* (4:1459).
30 Al-Subki, *Zafr al-amani* p. 422.

Among those who fall into the category of "Ibn Taymiyya and his followers" on this issue are:

* Ibn Abd al-Hadi who wrote *al-Sarim al-munki* in an attempt to refute Subki's book *Shifa al-siqam* on the great merit of visiting the Prophet (🌿);
* The "Salafi" author Bin Baz who said, "The hadith that concern the desirability of visiting the grave of the Prophet (🌿) are all weak, indeed forged" (*kulluha daifa bal mawdua*);[31]
* Nasir al-Din Albani, who claimed that the visit to the Prophet (🌿) ranks among the innovations.[32]
* Nasir al-Jadya, who in 1993 obtained his Ph.D. with First Honors from the University of Muhammad ibn Saud after writing a 600-page book entitled *al-Tabarruk* in which he perpetuates the same claim.[33]

One will find such books printed and distributed far and wide, while the classical books of mainstream Islam are deliberately ignored and made unavailable to Muslims at large.

Despite the claims of Wahhabis and "Salafis," the hadith "Whoever visits my grave is guaranteed my intercession" is one of the proof-texts adduced by the religious scholars (*ulama*) of Islam to demonstrate the obligation or recommendation of visiting the Prophet's grave and seeking him as an intermediary/means (*wasila*), as will be seen further down, in the chapter on visiting the Prophet's grave. Sakhawi said:

> The emphasis and encouragement on visiting his noble grave is mentioned in numerous hadith, and it would suffice to show this if there was only the hadith whereby the truthful and God-confirmed Prophet (🌿) promises that his intercession among other things becomes obligatory for whoever visits him, and the Imams are in complete agreement from the time directly after his passing until our own time that this

---

31 Bin Baz in the 1993 edition of *Fath al-bari* (3:387).
32 Nasir al-Din Albani, *Talkhis ankam al-janazi* p. 110 and elsewhere in his writings.
33 Nasir al-Jadya, *al-Tabarruk* p. 322.

[i.e. visiting him] is among the best acts of drawing near to Allah.[34]

Also:

• Muslim: "Whoever repeats after the words of the *muadhdhin*, my intercession is guaranteed for him."
• Tirmidhi (*hasan gharib*) and Ibn Hibban: "Those closest to me in the hereafter are those who invoked blessings upon me the most (in this world)."
• The Prophet (ﷺ) said, "My intercession is for those people of my Community who commit major sins." It is narrated by Tirmidhi (*hasan sahih gharib*), Abu Dawud, Ibn Majah, Ahmad, Ibn Hibban in his Sahih, and Abd al-Haqq Ibn al-Kharrat al-Ishbili cited it in *Kitab al-aqiba*. Ibn Hajar in *Fath al-bari* specified the following meaning of this hadith: "He did not restrict this to those who repented."[35]
• In Bukhari, from Imran ibn Husayn, whereby the Prophet (ﷺ) said, "A people will come out of the fire through the intercession of Muhammad, and will enter paradise. They will be called the *jahannamiyyun* (people of the fire)."
• In Muslim's *Sahih*: Abdullah ibn Amr ibn al-As narrated that the Prophet (ﷺ) recited the prayer of Abraham, "*My Lord! Lo! They have led many of mankind astray. But whoso followeth me, he verily is of me. And whoso disobeyeth me–still Thou art Forgiving, Merciful*" (14:36). Then he recited the saying of Jesus: "*If Thou punish them, lo! they are Thy slaves, and if Thou forgive them (lo! they are Thy slaves)*" (5:118). Then he raised his hands and said, "My Community, my Community!" and he wept. Allah said, "O Gabriel, go to Muhammad and ask him what causes him to weep." When Gabriel came and asked him he told him, upon which Gabriel returned and told Allah–Who knows better than him–and He said, "O Gabriel, go to Muhammad and tell him, 'We shall make thee glad concerning thy Community and We shall not displease you.'"[36]
• Tirmidhi (*hasan sahih*) and Ibn Majah: Abu ibn Kab narrated that the Prophet (ﷺ) said, "On the Day of Judgment I

34 Sakhawi, *al-Qawl al-badi* p. 160.
35 Ibn Hajar, *Fath al-bari*, Riqaq ch. 51 (1989 ed.) 11:522.
36 A reference to 93:5.

shall be the leader of prophets and their spokesman and the owner of their intercession and I say this without pride."[37]

• Tirmidhi (*hasan gharib*): From Anas, similar to the one before but applying to all people not only to prophets.

• Tirmidhi (*hasan gharib sahih*): Abu Hurayra narrates that the Prophet (ﷺ) said, "I shall stand before my Lord Glorious and Mighty and I shall be adorned with a garment from the garments of Paradise, after which I shall stand to the right of the Throne where none of creation will stand except myself."

• Tirmidhi (*gharib*): Ibn Abbas narrates:

> Some people close to the Prophet (ﷺ) came and waited for him. When he came out he approached them and heard them saying, "What a wonder it is that Allah Almighty and Glorious took one of His creation as His intimate Friend–Abraham (ﷺ)–while another one asked, "What is more wonderful than His speech to Moses (ﷺ), to whom He spoke directly!" Yet another one said, "And Jesus (ﷺ) is Allah's word and His spirit," while another one said, "Adam (ﷺ) was chosen by Allah." The Prophet (ﷺ) said, "I heard your words, and everything you said is indeed true. I myself am the Beloved of Allah (*habib Allah*). I say this without pride. I carry the flag of glory on the Day of Judgment, am the first intercessor, the first whose intercession is accepted, and the first to stir the circles of paradise so that Allah will open it for me. I shall enter it together with the poor among my Community. I say this without pride. I am the most honored of the first and the last and I say this without pride."

• Bukhari and Muslim: Jabir narrated that the Prophet (ﷺ) said, "I have been given five things which no Prophet (ﷺ) was given before me:

1 I was made victor over my enemies through fear struck in their heart.
2 I was permitted to take the booty of war.
3 The whole earth was made a place of prostration for me and its soil ritually pure, so when the time to pray

37 A reference to 4:41.

comes upon anyone of my Community, let him pray there and then.

4 I was given *shafaa* (intercession/mediation with Allah).

5 Every Prophet (🕮) was sent to his people in particular and I was sent to all peoples.

• Tirmidhi (*hasan*), Ibn Majah: Abu Said al-Khudri narrated that the Prophet (🕮) said, "I am the leader of human beings and I say this without pride. I am the first whom the earth will give up when it cleaves, and the first intercessor and the first whose intercession is accepted. I hold the flag of glory in my hand, and under it comes Adam and everyone else."

• Bukhari and Muslim: Anas and Abu Hurayra respectively narrate that the Prophet (🕮) said, "Every Prophet (🕮) has a request that is fulfilled, and I want to reserve my request of intercession for my Community on the Day of Judgment."

• Ahmad and Tabarani (*hasan*): Burayda narrates that the Prophet (🕮) said, "Verily I shall intercede on the Day of Judgment for more people than there are stones and clods of mud on the earth."

• Bukhari and Muslim: Abu Hurayra narrates a long hadith wherein the Prophet (🕮) intercedes and his intercession is accepted when all other prophets are powerless to intercede.

In al-Hasan's version in Bukhari, the Prophet (🕮) intercedes and is accepted four times:

• For those who have a grain of faith in their heart
• For those who have a mustard seed of faith in their heart
• For those who have less than that of faith in their heart
• For those who ever said, "There is no god but Allah (*la ilaha illallah*)"

1.4.2. INTERCESSION OF SPECIAL MEMBERS OF THE PROPHET'S COMMUNITY

1.4.2.1. FOR THE LIVING IN THEIR LIFETIME

Bukhari [*istisqa*]: Anas narrated:

> Whenever drought threatened them, Umar ibn al-Khattab used to ask Allah for rain through the medi-

ation of al-Abbas ibn Abd al-Muttalib. He [Umar] used to say, "O Allah! We used to ask you through the means of our Prophet (ﷺ) and You would bless us with rain, and now we ask You through the means of our Prophet's uncle, so bless us with rain." And it would rain.

1.4.2.2. IN THE AFTERLIFE

Tirmidhi (*hasan*), Ibn Majah, and al-Hakim: Abu Umama narrated that the Prophet (ﷺ) said, "More men will enter paradise through the intercession of a certain man than there are people in the tribes of Rabiah and Mudar," and that the elders considered that this was Uthman ibn Affan.

Tirmidhi (*hasan sahih*), Ibn Majah, and al-Hakim (*sahih*): Abu Abi al-Jada narrated that the Prophet (ﷺ) said, "More men will enter paradise through the intercession of one man than there are people in the tribe of Banu Tamim." They asked him, "Other than you?" He said, "Other than me," and it was said Uways al-Qarani was meant.

1.4.3. INTERCESSION OF THE COMMON BELIEVERS AMONG THE PROPHET'S COMMUNITY
1.4.3.1. IN THEIR LIFETIME FOR THOSE WHO PASSED AWAY

• Muslim (*janaiz*): Aisha reports the Prophet (ﷺ) as saying, "If a company of Muslims numbering one hundred pray over a dead person, all of them interceding for him, their intercession for him will be accepted."

• Muslim (*janaiz*): Ibn Abbas said, "I have heard the Prophet (ﷺ) say, 'If any Muslim dies and forty men who associate nothing with Allah stand over his body in prayer, Allah will accept them as intercessors for him.'"

• Abu Dawud: Narrated Abu Hurayra: Ali ibn Shammakh said, I was present with Marwan who asked Abu Hurayra, "Did you hear how the Prophet (ﷺ) used to pray over the dead?". . . Abu Hurayra said, "O Allah, Thou art its Lord. Thou didst create it, Thou didst guide it to Islam, Thou hast taken its spirit, and Thou knowest best its inner nature and outer aspect. We have come as intercessors, so forgive him."[38]

Ahmad[39] and others: In many traditions the number of acceptable intercessors in the funeral prayer is reduced to three rows of men, even if the number is under forty. Nawawi says the scholars of *usul al-fiqh* adduce these traditions also.

1.4.3.2. IN THE AFTERLIFE

• Tirmidhi (*hasan*), al-Bazzar: Abu Said al-Khudri and Anas respectively narrate that the Prophet (ﷺ) said, "One will be told, 'Stand, O so-and-so, and make intercession,' and he will stand and make intercession for his tribe and his family and for one man or two men or more according to his works."

• The prayer (*dua*) that is recited in the funeral prayer of a non-adult: "O Allah, make him/her our forerunner, and make him for us a reward and a treasure, make him one who will intercede (*shafian*) and whose intercession is accepted (*mushaffaan*)."

In this prayer (*dua*) the believer is clearly asking for intercession from a person who has passed away; in fact we are asking for intercession from a child who has not done any deeds in this world at all. A version that specifically mentions intercession is in Nawawi's *Adhkar*.[40]

In fact every *janaza* prayer contains a request for the intercession of the deceased in the phrase *wa la tahrimna ajrahu* which means "and do not prevent his reward from reaching us."

Bukhari related that the Prophet (ﷺ) also said, "He whose three children died before the age of puberty, they will shield him from the hell-fire, or will make him enter paradise."

1.5. OVERVIEW OF THE EVENTS OF THE LAST DAY AT THE STAGE OF INTERCESSION

The following is quoted from Dr. Muhammad Abul Quasem's book *Salvation of the Soul and Islamic Devotions*: Islamic [belief] is that for salvation intercession will take place at two stages: on the Day of Judgment and after the sinners' entry into hell.

---

38 Abu Dawud, Book 20, Number 3194.
39 Book 4, Number 79-100.
40 In the chapter of the prayers for the dead and it is translated in Nuh Keller's *Reliance* in the section on Funerals.

On the Day of Judgment it will take place first before the divine questioning; it is the Prophet Muhammad (ﷺ) who will intercede first for the forgiveness of his community. Accepting this intercession, Allah will grant him permission to take to paradise through its right gate (al-bab al-ayman) built for them especially, all those people of his community who are entitled to it without giving an account of their actions.[41]

Then, following the weighing of actions in the balance the verdict of damnation will be passed to numerous groups of believers who commit major sins, intercessors, including all prophets, will intercede for the forgiveness of many of them. The Prophet (ﷺ) said, "My intercession is for those people of my Community who commit major sins."[42] Allah out of mercy will accept. . . and save a large number of sinners. This salvation is free from damnation.

The second stage of intercession is after the sinners become like coal as a result of constant burning in hell-fire for a long time.[43] When they are suffering thus, intercessors will pray to Allah for the rescue of many of them. The result of this will be Divine forgiveness for them before the end of their redemptive punishment. This is salvation after damnation.

Who will intercede in the Hereafter? Not only the angels and all prophets, but also those believers who have high status with Allah, such as saints, sufis, religious scholars, and other pious men [and women], will be able to intercede for others.[44]

May Allah send blessings and peace upon the Intercessor Brought Near to Him, our Master Muhammad, and upon his Family and Companions, and may He grant us His Prophet's intercession on the Day of Reckoning.

41 Bukhari, *Tafsir* 17:5; Muslim, *zuhd* 14; Tirmidhi, *qiyama* 10; Ahmad 2:436.

42 Tirmidhi, *qiyama* 11; Abu Dawud, *sunna* 31; Ibn Majah, *zuhd* 37; Ahmad 3:213; and others. See previous mention of this hadith.

43 Muslim, *iman* 306; Bukhari, *riqaq* 56; Ibn Majah, *zuhd* 37; Ahmad 3:79.

44 Muhammad Abul Quasem, *Salvation of the Soul and Islamic Devotions* (Kegan Paul International 1981) p. 44.

2. SEEKING MEANS OF APPROACH TO ALLAH (*TAWASSUL*) THROUGH PROPHET MUHAMMAD (ﷺ)

awassul through the Prophet (ﷺ) is requested in acknowledgment of his status as the community's chief intercessor before Allah. It is a request for Allah's blessing as given by Allah through His Prophet (ﷺ) and His saints, and not as given by the Prophet (ﷺ) or saints alone, as those who oppose *tawassul* falsely impute. Allah has said of His Holy Prophet (ﷺ):

> *He is anxious about what you do, and merciful with the believers (9:128).*

> *If they had only, when they were unjust to themselves, come unto thee and asked Allah's forgiveness, and the Messenger had asked forgiveness for them, they would have found Allah indeed Oft-Returning, Most Merciful (4:64).*

> *And if they had had patience till thou camest forth unto them, it had been better for them. And Allah is Forgiving, Merciful (49:5).*

> *If only they had been content with what Allah and His Apostle gave them, and had said, "Sufficient unto us is Allah! Allah and His Apostle will soon give us of His bounty: to Allah do we turn our hopes!" (9:59).*

> *They swear by Allah to you (Muslims) in order to*

*please you: But it is more fitting that they should
please Allah and His Apostle, if they are believers
(9:62).*

Allah has mentioned all this about His Prophet (ﷺ) because
it is through His Prophet (ﷺ) that He Himself has shown His
greatest mercy and most comprehensive forgiveness, and it is
by coming to the Prophet (ﷺ) that the believers seek to obtain
these from Allah. This is clear evidence, now as it was then,
that the intervention of the Prophet (ﷺ) can be sought to obtain
forgiveness from Allah. The first hadith Imam Ahmad related
from Anas ibn Malik in his *Musnad* is: "The whole Community
of the people of Madina used to take the hand of the Prophet
(ﷺ) and rush to obtain their need with it."[1]

The *mufti* of Makka at the time of the spread of the
Wahhabi heresy, al-Sayyid Ahmad Ibn Zayni Dahlan (d. 1304)
said in *Khulasat al-kalam*:

> *Tawassul* (using means), *tashaffu* (using interces-
> sion), and *istighatha* (asking for help) all have the
> same meaning, and the only meaning they have in the
> hearts of the believers is that of *tabarruk* (using bless-
> ings) with the mention of Allah's beloved ones, since it
> is established that He grants His mercy to all His ser-
> vants for the sake of His beloved ones, and this is the
> case whether they are alive or dead, because in either
> case the actual effecting agent and true executor is
> Allah Himself, and these beloved ones are only ordi-
> nary causes for His mercy. Like any other secondary
> causes, they have no effective power of influence in
> themselves.[2]

The early and late Imams of the Community have said
clearly and unequivocally that *tawassul* through the Prophet
(ﷺ) is highly desirable and recommended for every person.
Following are some of their words to this effect.

> Imam Malik was asked the following question by
> the Caliph Abu Jafar al-Mansur: "Shall I face the
> *qibla* with my back towards the grave of the
> Messenger of Allah when making supplication (after

---

1 Ahmad, *Musnad* 3:98 (#11947).
2 Ahmad Zayni Dahlan, *Khulasat al-kalam fi umara al-balad al-haram* (The summation concerning the leaders of the sacrosanct country) 2:245.

salam)?" He replied: "How could you turn your face away from him when he is the means (wasila) of your and your father Adam's forgiveness from Allah on the Day of Resurrection? Nay, face him and ask for his intercession (istashfi bihi) so that Allah will grant it to you as He said, 'If they had only, when they were wronging themselves, come unto thee and asked Allah's forgiveness, and the Messenger had asked forgiveness for them, they would have found Allah indeed Oft-Returning, Most Merciful '(4:64)."

It is cited by al-Qadi Iyad with a sound (sahih) chain, and also by Samhudi, Subki, Qastallani, Ibn Jamaa, and Haytami. Ibn Jamaa says in Hidayat al-salik (3:1381): "It is related by the two hafiz Ibn Bashkuwal and al-Qadi Iyad in al-Shifa after him, and no attention is paid to the words of those who claim that it is forged purely on the basis of their idle desires."[3]

The words "He is the means (wasila) to Allah for your and your father Adam's forgiveness," are confirmed by verses where the Prophet (ﷺ) is witness over all communities and people, including their prophets:

> Thus, have We made of you an ummat justly balanced, that ye might be witnesses over the nations, and the Messenger a witness over yourselves; and We appointed the qibla to which thou wast used, only to test those who followed the Messenger from those who would turn on their heels (From the Faith). Indeed it was (a change) momentous, except to those guided by Allah. And never would Allah Make your faith of no effect. For Allah is to all people Most surely full of kindness, Most Merciful (2:143).[4]

> When Allah made (His) covenant with the prophets, (He said,) 'Behold that which I have given you of the Scripture and knowledge. And afterward there will come unto you a messenger, confirming that which ye possess. Ye shall believe in him and ye shall help him. He said, "Do ye agree, and will ye take up

---

3 It is cited by al-Qadi Iyad in al-Shifa (2:92-93) with a sound (sahih) chain, and also cited by Samhudi in Khulasat al-wafa, Subki in Shifa al-siqam, Qastallani in al-Mawahib al-laduniyya, Ibn Jamaa in Hidayat al-salik, and Haytami in al-Jawhar al-munazzam and Tuhfat al-zuwwar. See also Ibn Abd al-Hadi in al-Sarim al-munki p. 244 and Ibn Jamaa Hidayat al-salik (3:1381).
4 Yusuf Ali translation.

> My burden (which I lay upon you) in this (matter)?"
> They answered, "We agree." He said, "Then bear ye
> witness. I will be a witness with you" (3:81).

> But how (will it be with them) when We bring of
> every people a witness, and We bring thee (O
> Muhammad) a witness against these? (4:41)

> And when We exacted a covenant from the
> prophets, and from thee (O Muhammad) and from
> Noah and Abraham and Moses and Jesus son of Mary.
> We took from them a solemn covenant (33:7).[5]

This is also confirmed by the sound hadith concerning the Prophet's intercession before all prophets on behalf of all believers.[6] Finally, that Adam has been forgiven is established in the verse, "And Adam received words from his Lord and He relented towards him" (2:37).

Imam Ahmad made *tawassul* through the Prophet (ﷺ) a part of every supplication (*dua*) according to the following report: Ala al-Din al-Mardawi said:[7]

> The correct position of the [Hanbali] school of law
> is that it is permissible in one's supplication (*dua*) to
> use as one's means a pious person, and it is said that
> it is desirable (*mustahabb*). Imam Ahmad said to Abu
> Bakr al-Marwazi, "Let him use the Prophet (ﷺ) as a
> means in his supplication to Allah (*yatawassalu bi al-
> nabi fi duaih*)."

The same report is found in Imam Ahmad's *Manasik* as narrated by his student Abu Bakr al-Marwazi.

Similarly the lengthy wording of the *tawassul* according to the Hanbali school of law, as established by the *hafiz* Ibn Aqil in his *Tadhkira*, was cited fully by Imam Kawthari.[8]

2.1. PROPHET ADAM'S *TAWASSUL* THROUGH PROPHET MUHAMMAD (ﷺ)

The Prophet (ﷺ) said on the authority of Umar,

---

5 Pickthall translation.

6 *Sahih al-Bukhari* (*Kitab al-tawhid*).

7 Ahmad ibn Hanbal, *al-Insaf fi marifat al-rajih min al-khilaf ala madhhab al-imam al-mubajjal* (3:456).

8 Imam Kawthari in his appendix to Shaykh al-Islam Taqi al-Din al-Subki's *al-Sayf al-saqil* included in Kawthari's edition of the latter.

'When Adam (☙) committed his mistake he said, "O
my Lord, I am asking you to forgive me for the sake of
Muhammad." Allah said, "O Adam, and how do you
know about Muhammad whom I have not yet created?" Adam (☙) replied, "O my Lord, after You created
me with your hand and breathed into me of Your
Spirit, I raised my head and saw written on the
heights of the Throne, "There is no god but Allah and
Muhammad is the Messenger of Allah (la ilaha illallah muhammadun rasulullah).' I understood that You
would not place next to Your Name but the Most
Beloved One of Your creation." Allah said, 'O Adam, I
have forgiven you, and were it not for Muhammad I
would not have created you.'

The above text was transmitted through many chains and
was cited by Bayhaqi (in *Dalail al-nubuwwa*), Abu Nuaym (in
Dalail al-nubuwwa), al-Hakim in *al-Mustadrak* (2:615), al-
Tabarani in his *Saghir* (2:82, 207) with another chain contain-
ing sub-narrators unknown to Haythami as he stated in
Majma al-zawaid (8:253), and Ibn Asakir on the authority of
Umar ibn al-Khattab.[9]

This hadith is declared sound (*sahih*) by al-Hakim in *al-
Mustadrak* (2:651), although he acknowledges Abd al-Rahman
ibn Zayd ibn Aslam, one of its sub-narrators, as weak.
However, when he mentions this hadith he says, "Its chain is
sound, and it is the first hadith of Abd al-Rahman ibn Zayd ibn
Aslam which I mention in this book." Al-Hakim also declares
sound another version through Ibn Abbas.

Al-Bulqini declares this hadith sound in his *Fatawa*.

Al-Subki confirms al-Hakim's authentication (in *Shifa al-
siqam fi ziyarat khayr al-anam* p. 134-135) although Ibn
Taymiyya's rejection and criticism of this hadith was known to
him and he rejects it, saying that Ibn Taymiyya's extreme
weakening of Ibn Zayd is exaggerated.

The hadith is also included by Qadi Iyad among the "sound
and famous narrations" in *al-Shifa*, and he says that Abu
Muhammad al-Makki and Abu al-Layth al-Samarqandi mention it. Qadi Iyad says, "It is said that this hadith explains the

---

9 Most of these narrations were copied in Qastallani's *al-Mawahib al-laduniyya*
(and al-Zarqani's Commentary 2:62).

verse, 'And Adam received words from his Lord and He relented towards him' (2:37)." He continues to cite another very similar version through al-Ajurri (d. 360), about whom al-Qari
said, "Al-Halabi said, 'This seems to be the imam and guide
Abu Bakr Muhammad ibn al-Husayn ibn Abd Allah al-
Baghdadi, the compiler of the books al-Sharia devoted to the
sunna, al-Arbaun, and others.'" This is confirmed by Ibn
Taymiyya in his Qaida fi al-tawassul: "It is related by Shaykh
Abu Bakr al-Ajurri, in his book al-Sharia."

Ibn al-Jawzi also considers it sound (sahih) as he cites it in
the first chapter of al-Wafa bi ahwal al-mustafa, in the introduction of which he says, "(In this book) I do not mix the sound
hadith with the false," although he knew of Abd al-Rahman ibn
Zayd's weakness as a narrator; he also mentions the version of
Maysarat al-fajr whereby the Prophet (ﷺ) says, "When satan
deceived Adam and Eve, they repented and sought intercession
from Allah with my name." Ibn al-Jawzi also says in the chapter concerning the Prophet's superiority over the other
prophets in the same book, "Part of the exposition of his superiority to other prophets is the fact that Adam asked his Lord
through the sanctity (hurma) of Muhammad that He relent
towards him, as we have already mentioned."

Suyuti cites it in his Quranic commentary al-Durr al-manthur (2:37) and in al-Khasais al-Kubra (1:12) and in al-Riyad
al-aniqa fi sharh asma khayr al-khaliqa (p. 49), where he says
that Bayhaqi considers it sound. This is due to the fact that
Bayhaqi said in the introduction to the Dalail that he only
included sound narrations in his book, although he also knew
and explicitly mentions Abd al-Rahman ibn Zayd's weakness.

Ibn Kathir mentions it after Bayhaqi in al-Bidaya wal-
nihaya (1:75, 1:180).

Al-Haythami in Majma al-zawaid (8:253 #28870), Bayhaqi
himself, and al-Qari in Sharh al-shifa show that its chains
have weakness in them. However, the weakness of Abd al-
Rahman ibn Zayd was known by Ibn al-Jawzi, Subki, Bayhaqi,
Hakim, and Abu Nuaym, yet all these scholars retained this
hadith for consideration in their books.

Three scholars reject it, such as Ibn Taymiyya (Qaida jalila
fi al-tawassul p. 89, 168-170) and his two students Ibn Abd al-
Hadi (al-Sarim al-munki p. 61-63) and al-Dhahabi (Mizan al-

itidal 2:504 and *Talkhis al-mustadrak*), while Asqalani reports Ibn Hibban's saying that Abd al-Rahman ibn Zayd was a forger (*Lisan al-mizan* 3:360, 3:442).

At the same time, Ibn Taymiyya elsewhere quotes this version and one through Maysara and says, "These two are like the elucidation (*tafsir*) of the authentic *ahadith* (concerning the same topic)" (*Fatawa* 2:150). The contemporary Makkan hadith scholar Ibn Alawi al-Maliki said, "This indicates that Ibn Taymiyya found the hadith sound enough to be considered a witness for other narrations (*salih li al-istishhad wa al-itibar*), because the forged (*al-mawdu*) and the false (*al-batil*) are not taken as witness by the people of hadith." Al-Maliki also quotes (without reference) Dhahabi's unrestrained endorsement of the hadith in Bayhaqi's *Dalail al-nubuwwa* with his words, "You must take what is in it (the *dalail*), for it consists entirely of guidance and light" (*Mafahim yajib an tusahhah* p. 47).

2.2. ALLAH'S CREATION FOR THE SAKE OF PROPHET MUHAMMAD (ﷺ)

It is furthermore evident that Ibn Taymiyya considers the meaning of the creation of everything for the sake of the Prophet (ﷺ) as true and correct, as he declares in his *Majmuat al-fatawa* in the volume on *tasawwuf* (11:95-97):

> Muhammad is the Chief of the Children of Adam, the Best of Creation, the noblest of them in the sight of Allah. This is why some have said that "Allah created the Universe due to him," or that "Were it not for him, He would have neither created a Throne, nor a Footstool, nor a heaven, earth, sun or moon." However, this is not a hadith on the authority of the Prophet (ﷺ) . . . but it may be explained from a correct aspect . . .
>
> Since the best of the righteous of the children of Adam (ﷺ) is Muhammad (ﷺ), creating him was a desirable end of deep-seated purposeful wisdom, more than for anyone else, and hence the completion of creation and the fulfillment of perfection was attained with Muhammad (ﷺ). The Chief of the Children of Adam (ﷺ) is Muhammad (ﷺ). Adam (ﷺ) and his children being under his banner. He said, "Truly, I was written as the Seal of the Prophets with Allah,

when Adam (🕮) was going to-and-fro in his clay," i.e. meaning that "my prophethood was decreed and manifested when Adam (🕮) was created but before the breathing of the Spirit into him," just as Allah decrees the livelihood, lifespan, deeds and misery or happiness of the slave when He creates the embryo but before the breathing of the Spirit into it.

Since man is the seal and last of all creation, and its microcosm, and since the best of man is thus the best of all creation absolutely, then Muhammad, being the Pupil of the Eye, the Axis of the Mill, and the Distributor to the Collective, is as it were the Ultimate Purpose from amongst all the purposes of creation. Thus it cannot be denied to say that "Due to him all of this was created", or that "Were it not for him, all this would not have been created;" if statements like this are thus explained according to what the Book and the *sunna* indicate, it is acceptable.

Its latter part is mentioned as a separate hadith in the wording, "Were it not for Muhammad, I would not have created the spheres (*al-aflak*)." Al-Ajluni said,[10] "Al-Saghani (d.650) said it is forged. I say, but its meaning is correct." Similarly, according to Ali al-Qari,[11] "Al-Saghani said,[12] 'It is forged,' however, its meaning is sound (*minahu sahih*), as Daylami has narrated on the authority of Ibn Abbas that the Prophet (🕮) said, "Gabriel came to me and said, O Muhammad! Were it not for you, paradise would not have been created, and were it not for you, the fire would not have been created." And Ibn Asakir transmits: "And were it not for you, the world would not have been created."

As for Albani's rejection of Qari's use of Daylami in support of the hadith with the words, "I do not hesitate to declare it weak on the basis that Daylami is alone in citing it" (*Silsila daifa* #282), it shows exaggeration and deviation from the practice of the scholars concerning Daylami and his book. Ibn Taymiyya said in *Minhaj al-sunna* (4:38): "The fact that Daylami alone narrates a hadith does not indicate that the hadith is sound." Note that he never said, "The fact that Daylami alone narrates a hadith indicates that it is forged," yet

---

10 Al-Ajluni, *Kashf al-khafa* (#2123).
11 Ali al-Qari, *al-Asrar al-marfua* (#754-755).
12 Al-Saghani, *al-Ahadith al-mawdua* p. 7.

this is what Albani concludes! The reader may compare Albani's method of a priori rejection in lieu of a discussion of the hadith itself, to Ibn Hajar al-Asqalani's reliance on a hadith narrated by Daylami, as is shown by hadith #33 of his *Arbaun fi rad al-mujrim an sabb al-muslim*, although Daylami is alone in citing it. Further, in *Minhaj al-sunna*, Ibn Taymiyya declared of him and his book, "Al-Daylami in his book *al-Firdaws* mentioned many sound (*sahih*) hadiths, and also fair (*hasan*) narrations and forged ones . . . He was one of the people of knowledge and religion and he was not a liar."[13]

Ibn al-Qayyim in his *Badai al-fawaid* went so far as to represent Allah saying to humankind that everything was created for the sake of human beings:

> Have you realized your value? I only created all the universes for your sake . . . All things are trees whose fruit you are (*hal arifat qimata nafsik? innama khalaqtu al-akwana kullaha laka . . . kullu ul-ushiyai shajaratun wa anta al-thamara*).[14]

If Allah created all the universes for the sake of human beings, then how could all humanity be given what the Prophet (ﷺ) is denied, who is better than mankind and *jinn* put together?

2.3. THE PROPHET'S NAME WRITTEN WITH ALLAH'S NAME

Following are some of the hadiths that mention the Prophet's name together with Allah's name on the Throne and in the heavens, which are cited by the hadith masters, as related by Suyuti:[15]

> • In Ibn Asakir from Kab al-Ahbar: Adam (ﷺ) said to his son Seth (ﷺ), "O my son, you are my successor, therefore found my successorhip upon Godwariness and the Firm Rope, and every time you mention Allah, do mention next to His name the name of Muhammad, for I saw his name written on the leg of the Throne as I was between the spirit and

13 Ibn Taymiyya, *Minhaj al-sunna* (4:78).
14 Ibn Qayyim al-Jawziyya, *Badai al-fawaid* (Alexandria: Dar al-dawa, 1412/1992) p. 63.
15 Suyuti, *al-Khasais al-kubra* (1:12-14).

the clay. Then I circumambulated the heavens and I did not see in them a single spot except the name of Muhammad was written upon it, and when my Lord made me inhabit paradise I saw in it neither palace nor room except the name of Muhammad was written on it. I have seen his name written on the bosom of the wide-eyed maidens of paradise, on the leaves of the reed-stalks and thickets of the garden, on the leaves of the tree of bliss, on the leaves of the Lote-tree of the Farthermost Boundary, and upon the veils and between the eyes of the angels. Therefore, make frequent remembrance of him, for the angels remember him in every moment."

• Ibn Adi and Ibn Asakir from Anas that the Prophet (ﷺ) said, "When I was taken up to heaven I saw written on the leg of the Throne: *'La ilaha illallah muhammadun rasulullah ayyadtuhu bi ali"* (there is no god but Allah and Muhammad is the Messenger of Allah and I have supported him with Ali).'"[16]

• Ibn Asakir from Ali that the Prophet (ﷺ) said, "The night I was enraptured I saw written on the Throne: *'La ilaha illallah muhammadun rasulullah Abu bakr al-siddiq umar al-faruq uthman dhu al-nurayn"* (there is no god but Allah and Muhammad is the Messenger of Allah, Abu Bakr al-Siddiq, Umar al-Faruq, Uthman of the Two Lights).'"[17]

• Ibn Adi, Tabarani in *al-Awsat*, Ibn Asakir, and al-Hasan ibn Arafa in his famous volume from Abu Hurayra that the Prophet (ﷺ) said, "The night I was enraptured and taken up to heaven I did not pass a heaven except I saw in it my name written, *'Muhammadun rasulullah '* with Abu Bakr at my side."

• Al-Bazzar from Ibn Umar: The Prophet (ﷺ) said, "When I was taken up to heaven I did not pass a heaven except I saw in it my name written,

---

16 See also al-Khatib (11:173) and Suyuti in *al-Durr al-manthur* (4:153). Al-Haythami cites it in *Majma al-zawaid* as narrated from the Companion Abul Hamra (Hilal ibn al-Harith), the servant of the Prophet, rather than Anas, and says: "Its chain contains Amr ibn Thabit and his narrations are abandoned (*matruk*)." This is different from Amr ibn Thabit al-Tabii (the student of Abd Allah ibn Umar), who is trustworthy (*thiqa*).

17 Also al-Khatib in *Tarikh Baghdad* (10:264) and Suyuti in *al-Durr al-manthur* (4:153) without the mention of the three caliphs.

'*Muhammadun rasulullah*" (Muhammad is the Messenger of Allah)."[18]

• Al-Khatib, Ibn Asakir, and al-Daraqutni in *al-Afrad* (reports from a single narrator), from Abu al-Darda that the Prophet (ﷺ) said, "The night I was enraptured I saw a green garment on the Throne whereupon was written in letters of light, '*La ilaha illallah muhammadun rasulullah abu bakr al-siddiq umar al-faruq* (there is no god but Allah and Muhammad is the Messenger of Allah, Abu Bakr al-Siddiq, Umar al-Faruq)'".

• Ibn Asakir from Jabir that the Prophet (ﷺ) said, "On the gate of Paradise is written, '*La ilaha illallah muhammadun rasulullah* (there is no god but Allah and Muhammad is the Messenger of Allah)."[19]

• Abu Nuaym in *al-Hilya* from Ibn Abbas that the Prophet (ﷺ) said, "There is not in all paradise one tree with a single leaf but inscribed, '*La ilaha illallah muhammadun rasulullah*" (There is no god but Allah and Muhammad is the Messenger of Allah)."[20]

• Al-Hakim from Ibn Abbas, and he graded it *sahih* (sound), "Allah revealed to Jesus (ﷺ) the following, "Believe in Muhammad and order all those of your Community who see him to believe in him, for were it not for Muhammad I would not have created Adam, nor paradise, nor the fire. When I created the Throne upon the water it shuddered. So I wrote upon it, "*La ilaha illallah muhammadun rasulullah* (there is no god but Allah and Muhammad is the Messenger of Allah) and it became calm.'" Al-Dhahabi said, "Its

---

18 Al-Haythami said in *Majma al-zawaid*: "From Ibn Umar: The Prophet said: "When I was taken up to heaven, in every heaven that I passed, I saw in it my name written: Muhammad is the Messenger of Allah Abu Bakr al-Siddiq (*muhammadun rasullah abu bakr al-siddiq*)." Its chain contians Abd Allah ibn Ibrahim al-Ghifari who is weak."

19 Al-Haythami in *Majma al-zawaid* narrates it with the additon: *ali akhu al-nabi sallallahu alayhi wa sallama qabla an yakhluqa al-khalq* (in another version: *qabla an yakhluqa al-samawati wa al-ard) bi alfay sanatin*. Haythami says: "Tabarani narrated it in *al-Awsat* and its chain contains al-Ashath ibn Amm al-Hasan ibn Salih who is weak, and I do not know him."

20 Al-Haytham in *Majma al-zawaid* says: "In Tabarani from Ibn Abbas: The Prophet said, "There is a tree in paradise" or "There is no tree in paradise," the narrator, Ali ibn Jumayl, was unsure, "except all of its leaves are inscribed: *la ilaha illallah muhammadun rasulullah abu bakr al-siddiq umar al-faruq uthman dhu al-nurayn*. Tabarani narrates it and its chain contains Ali ibn Jumayl who is weak."

chain contains Amr ibn Aws and it is not known who
he is."[21]

• In Ibn Asakir from Jabir through Abu al-Zubayr,
"Between Adam's shoulders is written, '*Muhammadun rasulullah khatam al-nabiyyin* (Muhammad
is the Messenger of Allah, the Seal of the Prophets).'"

Imam Shawkani said in his commentary on al-
Jazari's (d. 833) *Iddat al-hisn al-hasin* entitled *Tuhfat
al-dhakirin bi iddat al-hisn al-hasin*:[22] "He [al-
Jazari] said, 'Let him make *tawassul* to Allah with
His prophets and the *salihin* or saints (in his supplication).' I say that exemplifying *tawassul* with the
prophets is the hadith extracted by Tirmidhi et al. (of
the blind man saying, "O Allah, I ask You and turn to
You by means of Muhammad (ﷺ) the Prophet of
Mercy)"[23] . . . As for *tawassul* with the saints, among
its examples is the hadith (established as sound) of
the Companions' *tawassul*, asking Allah for rain by
means of al-Abbas, the Prophet's uncle; Umar said, "O
Allah, we use as means to You the uncle of our
Prophet (ﷺ) etc . . ."[24] Shawkani's complete and
detailed stand on *tawassul* from his treatise *al-Durr
al-nadir* is cited further below.

2.4. THE HADITH OF THE BLIND MAN'S INTERCESSION THROUGH PROPHET MUHAMMAD (ﷺ)

A blind man went to the Prophet (ﷺ) and said,
"Invoke Allah for me that he help me." He replied, "If
you wish I will delay this, and it would be better for
you, and if you wish I will invoke Allah the Exalted
(for you)." He said, "Then invoke him." The Prophet
(ﷺ) said to him, '*Idhhab fa tawadda, wa salli rakat-
tayn thumma qul* (go and make an ablution, offer two
cycles of prescribe prayer (*salat*), then say, "O Allah, I
am asking you (*asaluka*) and turning to you (*atawajjahu ilayka*) with your Prophet Muhammad (ﷺ) (*bi*

21 No doubt this is other than Amr ibn Aws al-Thaqafi the great *tabii* whose narrations are found in Bukhari and Muslim.
22 Shawkani, commentary on *Iddat al-hisn al-hasin* entitled *Tuhfat al-dhakirin
bi iddat al-hisn al-hasin* Beirut ed. 1970, p. 37.
23 See below, next page.
24 See below, next paragraph.

nabiyyika muhammad), the Prophet of mercy; O Muhammad (ﷺ) (*ya Muhammad*), I am turning with you to my Lord regarding my present need. I am asking my Lord with your intercession concerning the return of my sight (*inni atawajjahu bika ila rabbi fi hajati hadhih*–another version has: *inni astashfiu bika ala rabbi fi raddi basari*)' so that He will fulfill my need. 'O Allah, allow him to intercede (with you) for me (*allahumma shaffihu fiyya*)."""[25]

The Prophet's order, here as elsewhere, carries legislative force for all Muslims and is not limited to a particular person, place or time; it is valid for all generations until the end of time unless proven otherwise by a subsequent indication from the Prophet (ﷺ) himself.

The Prophet (ﷺ) was not physically present at the assigned time of the invocation, since he said to the blind man, "Go and make ablution," without adding, "and then come back in front of me." With regard to physical absence, the living and the dead are exactly alike; namely, absent.

Despite the Prophet's physical absence, the wording (*sigha*) for calling upon his intercession is direct address: "O Muhammad." Such wording–"O so-and-so"–is only used with someone present and able to hear. It should also be noted that Allah forbade the Companions from being forward or calling out to the Prophet (ﷺ) in the ordinary manner used with one another (49:1-2). The only way, therefore, that the Prophet (ﷺ) could both be absent and at the same be addressed is that the first be understood in the physical sense and the second in the spiritual.

The above invocation was also used after the Prophet's lifetime, as is proven by the sound (*sahih*) hadith authenticated by Bayhaqi, Abu Nuaym,[26] Mundhiri,[27] Haythami, and Tabarani.[28] They relate, on the authority of Uthman ibn Hunayf's nephew Abu Imama ibn Sahl ibn Hunayf:

---

25 It is related by Ahmad (4:138 #17246-17247), Tirmidhi (*hasan sahih gharib*, *Daawat* Ch. 119), Ibn Majah (Book of *Iqamat al-salat wal-sunnat*, Ch. on *Salat al-hajat* #1385), Nasai (*Amal al-yawm wal-laylat* p. 417-418 #658-660), al-Hakim (1:313,1:526), Tabarani in *al-Kabir*, and rigorously authenticated as sound (*sahih*) by nearly fifteen hadith masters including Ibn Hajar, Dhahabi, Shawkani, and Ibn Taymiyya.

26 Abu Nuaym, *Marifa*.

27 Mundhiri, *Targhib* 1:473-474.

28 Tabarani in the *Kabir* (9:17-18) and the *Saghir* (1:184/201-202).

A man would come to Uthman ibn Affan for a certain need, but the latter would not pay him any attention nor look into his need, upon which he complained
of his condition to Uthman ibn Hunayf who told him,
"Go and make ablution, then go to the mosque and
pray two cycles (*rakat*), then say this supplication
(*dua*)," and he mentioned the invocation of the blind
man, "then go (to Uthman again)." The man went, did
as he was told, then came to Uthman's door, to which
the door attendant came, took him by the hand, and
brought him to Uthman Ibn Affan who sat with him
on top of the carpet, and said, "Tell me what your need
is." After this the man went out, met Uthman ibn
Hunayf again, and said to him, "May Allah reward
you! Previously he would not look into my need nor
pay any attention to me, until you spoke to him." He
replied, "I did not speak to him, but I saw the Prophet
(ﷺ) when a blind man came to him complaining of his
failing eyesight," and he mentioned to him the sub-
stance of the previous narration.

2.5. UMAR'S *TAWASSUL* FOR RAIN THROUGH THE PROPHET'S UNCLE

It is narrated that Umar ibn al-Khattab, the second caliph,
would pray to Allah for rain during times of drought through
the means, the honor and intercession of the uncle of the
Prophet (ﷺ), Abbas ibn Abd Muttalib by using this supplication: "O Our Lord! Previously, when we had a drought, we used
to come to You by means and intercession of Your Prophet (ﷺ).
Now we are requesting intercession through the uncle of the
Prophet (ﷺ) to grant us rain," and it was granted. Bukhari
relates it. Umar added, after making this supplication:"*hadha
wallahi al-wasilatu ilallahi azza wa jall*" (He (al-Abbas), by
Allah, is the means to Allah).[29]

The scholars say that Umar sought the means of al-Abbas
rather than the Prophet (ﷺ) in order to show and acknowledge
the status of the Prophet's uncle among the people and, more
generally, of the *Ahl al-Bayt* or direct relatives of the Prophet
(ﷺ). Kawthari cites Ibn Abd al-Barr's commentary in *al-Istiab*
that Umar used al-Abbas in response to Kab's words, "O

29 Ibn Abd al-Barr relates it in *al-Istiab bi marifat al-ashab*.

Commander of the believers, the Bani Israil in such circumstances used to pray for rain by means of the relatives of prophets."[30] It is not, as some have fancied, because the Prophet's means is no longer available that Umar used al-Abbas as a *wasila*. The hadith of Uthman ibn Hunayf and the words of Malik to al-Mansur show that the Prophet (ﷺ) continued to be sought by the Companions and Followers as a means of benefit even after he left this life.

The following is more evidence to this effect:

2.6. AISHA'S *TAWASSUL* FOR RAIN THROUGH THE PROPHET (ﷺ)

> Al-Darimi relates from Aws ibn Abd Allah with a good chain:[31] "The people of Madina complained to Aisha of the severe drought that they were suffering. She said, 'Go to the Prophet's grave and open a window towards the sky so that there will be no roof between him and the sky.' They did so, after which they were watered with such rain that vegetation grew and the camels got fat. That year was named the Year of Plenty."

It is clear from the above narrations that the position of the Mother of the Believers, Aisha, differs from that of modern-day "Salafis," since she recommended to the people of Madina to use the Prophet (ﷺ) in his grave as a means of obtaining blessing and benefit. This practice continued until the Wahhabis took over the Hijaz but the "Salafis" continue to denounce this as unacceptable.

Albani, in an effort to reject the hadith of Darimi, raised some objections that are faulty. He said the following about Darimi's chain of transmission (Abu al-Numan from Said ibn Zayd from Amr ibn Malik al-Nukri from Abu al-Jawza Aws ibn Abd Allah from Aisha):[32]

> This chain of narration is weak and cannot be used as a proof due to three reasons:
> (i) Said ibn Zayd who is the brother of Hammad

---

30 Kawthari, *Maqalat* p. 411.

31 Al-Darimi in Ch. 15 of the *Muqaddima* (Introduction) to *Sunan* (1:43) entitled: "Allah's generosity to His Prophet after his death."

32 Albani, *Tawassul: Its Types and Its Rulings* (p. 130-131).

ibn Zayd is somewhat weak. *Al-hafiz* [Ibn Hajar] said about him in *al-Taqrib*, "Generally acceptable, but he makes mistakes." Dhahabi said about him in *al-Mizan*, "Yahya ibn Said said, 'Weak,' and al-Sadi said, 'He is not a proof, they declare his ahadith to be weak.' Nasai and others said, 'He is not strong.' Ahmad said, 'He is all right.' Yahya ibn Said would not accept him.'"

The above documentation is partial, biased, and demonstrates the "Salafi" tendency not to mention anything that may contradict their views. This is especially true of Albani. Despite the claim of Albani's followers that he is the "leading scholar of hadith of this age," he makes frequent mistakes, innovates in many of his rulings, and is generally unreliable.

The present narration is a case in point. Albani neglects to mention the authentication of the narrators he declares weak, thus hiding basic evidence from his readers, and misleading them in order to support his sect's rejection of the concept of intercession. The following is a point-by-point refutation of Albani's claims by the Moroccan hadith scholar Abd Allah ibn Muhammad ibn al-Siddiq al-Ghumari:[33]

Albani's weakening of Said ibn Zayd is rejected, because Said is one of Muslim's narrators, and Yahya ibn Main declared him trustworthy (*thiqa*)!

The editor of Ghumari's text, Ghumari's student Hasan Ali al-Saqqaf says on the same page as the above:

Albani has adduced worthless proofs as is his habit when embellishing falsehood. He cited whatever fit his whim from Ibn Hajar's *Taqrib*, leaving out his mention that Said ibn Zayd is one of Muslim's narrators in his *Sahih*. Beware, therefore, of this *tadlis* (concealment) on his part! . . . He added Dhahabi's notice on Said ibn Zayd in the *Mizan*, and this is another deliberate cover-up, for he faithlessly omitted to mention what Ibn Hajar reported in *Tahdhib al-*

tahdhib (4:29) from those who declared Said ibn Zayd trustworthy (in addition to his being one of Muslim's narrators):
  • Bukhari said, "Muslim ibn Ibrahim narrated to us: Said ibn Zayd Abu al-Hasan narrated to us, and he is reliable and a memorizer of hadith (*saduq hafiz*)."
  • Al-Duri said on the authority of Ibn Main, "Said ibn Zayd is trustworthy (*thiqa*)."
  • Ibn Sad said, "He was trustworthy."
  • Al-Ujli said, "He is from Basra, and he is trustworthy."
  • Abu Zura said, "I heard Sulayman ibn Harb say: Said ibn Zayd narrated to us, and he was trustworthy."
  • Abu Jafar al-Darimi said, "Hibban ibn Hilal narrated to us: Said ibn Zayd narrated to us, and he was a memorizer of hadith and he was reliable."
  • Ibn Adi said, "There is no denounced narration from him except someone else also narrates it, and I consider him one of those in the reliable category."

In addition to the above remarks it is noteworthy to mention that Albani cited Ahmad's grading of Said ibn Zayd as *la basa bihi* which his translator rendered as "he is all right," but neither the author nor the translator acknowledges that in Imam Ahmad's terminology *la basa bihi* is identical with *thiqa*, which means "trustworthy" and is among the highest gradings of authentication! Ibn Salah,[34] Dhahabi,[35] Sakhawi,[36] Ibn Hajar,[37] Abu Ghudda,[38] as well as the editor of Nawawi's *al-Taqrib wa al-taysir*,[39] have indicated that the equivalency of saying "There is no harm in him" with the grade of trustworthy (*thiqa*) obtains for many early authorities of the third century such as Ibn Main, Ibn al-Madini, Imam Ahmad, Duhaym, Abu Zura, Abu Hatim al-Razi, Yaqub ibn Sufyan al-Fasawi, and others.

Albani continues in his list of reasons for weakening Darimi's narration:

(ii) It is *mawquf* (stopping at the Companion),

---

34 Ibn Salah, *Muqaddima* (p. 134).
35 Dhahabi, *Lisan al-mizan* (1:13).
36 Sakhawi, *Fath al-mughith*.
37 Ibn Hajar, *Hadi al-sari*.
38 Abu Ghudda in his commentary to Lucknawi's *Raf* (p. 222 n3).
39 Nawawi, *al-Taqrib wa al-taysir* p. 51.

coming only from Aisha and not from the Prophet (ﷺ), and even if the chain of narration up to Aisha were authentic, it would not be a proof since it is something open to personal judgment in which even the Companions are sometimes correct and sometimes incorrect, and we are not bound to act upon that.

To this claim, it is easy to reply that not only is the narration sound and authentic, but also that there is no reported objection by any of the Companions to the act recommended by the Mother of the Believers, just as there was no objection on their part to the *istisqa* made by the man who came to the grave of the Prophet (ﷺ) in the narration of Malik al-Dar cited below. This shows *ijma* on the matter on the part of the Companions, and such *ijma* is definitely binding in the sense that no one can declare unlawful or innovative something which they have tacitly declared lawful or desirable. In regard to following the opinion of the Companions, Imam al-Shafii said, "Their opinion for us is better than our opinion to ourselves."[40]

Albani listed the following as his last reason for weakening Darimi's narration:

(iii) Abu al-Numan . . . was originally a reliable narrator except that he deteriorated at the end of his life. The hadith master Burhan al-Din al-Halabi mentions him among those who deteriorated in later life in his book *al-Muqaddima* (p. 391) and he says, "The ruling about these people is that their narrations are accepted if reported from them by people who heard from them before they deteriorated. But narrations reported from them by those who heard from them after they deteriorated, or narrations reported from them by people about whom we do not know whether they heard from them before they deteriorated or after, then these narrations are to be rejected."

I say that we do not know whether this report was heard by Darimi from him before or after his memory deteriorated, it is therefore not acceptable and cannot be used as evidence. [Footnote] Shaykh al-Ghumari missed this weakness in *Misbah al-zujaj* (p. 43), just

---

40 As related by Ibn Qayyim in *Ilam al-muwaqqiin an rabb al-alamin* (2:186-187).

as it was ignored by another in order to give the impression to the people that this report is authentic.

Ghumari said regarding these claims about Abu al-Numan:

His weakening of Abu al-Numan is invalid, because Abu al-Numan's deterioration did not affect what is narrated from him! Al-Daraqutni said [as cited by Dhahabi in *Mizan al-itidal* (4:81)], "He deteriorated at the end of his life, and no denounced hadith issued from him after his deterioration whatsoever, and he is trustworthy (*thiqa*)." As for what Ibn Hibban said: "Many denounced things occurred in his narrations after his deterioration," al-Dhahabi refuted it when he said (4:8), "Ibn Hibban was unable to cite a single denounced narration from him, and the truth is just as Daraqutni said."

Shaykh Muhammad ibn Alawi al-Maliki said:[41]

Abu al-Numan's deterioration neither harms nor is detrimental to his reliability, since Bukhari in his *Sahih* narrated over one hundred hadiths from him, and no narration was taken from him after his deterioration, as Daraqutni said . . . The chain of transmission is all right, in fact I consider it good. The scholars have cited as evidence many chains that are like it or less strong than it.

Following are Saqqaf's further comments, beginning with Albani's charge against Shaykh al-Ghumari:

We know full well that it is Albani who betrays scholarly trust and deliberately misinforms the people, even if he accuses others of misinformation . . . In weakening Abu al-Numan he has again acted faithlessly. His quotation from al-Burhan al-Halabi's book *al-Ightibat bi man rumiya bi al-ikhtilat* (p. 23) is designed to pull the wool over the eyes of his followers and those who only read his works! For it is necessary to also know that those who are branded as suffering from deterioration in the aforementioned

41 Shaykh Muhammad ibn Alawi al-Maliki in his book *Shifa al-fuad bi ziyarat khayr al-iban* (p. 152).

book are divided among those whose narrations were
unaffected by their deterioration and those whose
narrations were affected. Abu al-Numan belongs to
the first group, and al-Dhahabi made this clear in *al-
Mizan* (4:8). Therefore our reply to Albani is: Shaykh
al-Ghumari did not miss anything concerning this
matter of deterioration, because he is a hadith scholar and a master memorizer (*hafiz*), however, it is you
who have missed it, O slandering backbiter!

As for Albani's quotation of Ibn Taymiyya's claim that "a
clear proof that it is a lie is the fact that no such opening exist-
ed above the house at all in the whole of the life of Aisha,"[42] it
is a weak objection that is no sooner brought up than cast out.
Surely Imam al-Darimi and the scholars of the succeeding generations would know of such a detail better than latecomers.
Even authorities among the latter dismiss Albani's objections.
For example, the hadith scholar and historian of Madina Imam
Ali al-Samhudi (d. 922) did not so much as look at Ibn
Taymiyya's objection. Rather, he confirmed the truth of
Darimi's narration by saying,[43] al-Zayn al-Miraghi said, "Know
that it is the *sunna* of the people of Madina to this day to open
a window at the bottom of the dome of the Prophet's room, that
is, of the blessed green dome, on the side of the *qibla*." I say,
And in our time, they open the door facing the noble face (the
grave) in the space surrounding the room and they gather
there."

The act of the Mother of the Believers, Aisha, in the narration of Darimi is explicitly confirmed by Abu Talib's famous line
of poetry concerning *istisqa* through the Prophet (ﷺ) as related in the book of *istisqa* in Bukhari's *Sahih*:

2.7 THE PROPHET'S PRAYER FOR RAIN (*ISTISQA*)

Abdullah ibn Dinar said, "I heard Ibn Umar recit-
ing the poetic verses of Abu Talib:

A fair-skinned one by whose face rainclouds are
sought,

42 Ibn Taymiyya, *al-Radd ala al-bakri* (p. 68-74).
43 Albani after citing Ibn Taymiyya in his *Wafa al-wafa* (2:549).

A caretaker for the orphans and protector of widows.

Umar ibn Hamza said, Salim narrated from his father (Ibn Umar) that the latter said, "The poet's saying came to my mind as I was looking at the face of the Prophet (ﷺ) while he was praying for rain–and he did not get down till the rain water flowed profusely from every roof-gutter:
A fair-skinned one by whose face rainclouds are
    sought,
A caretaker for the orphans and protector of widows.

One sub-narrator added, "These were the words of Abu Talib."

Note that in his translation of Bukhari, Muhammad Muhsin Khan alters the wording of the hadith to read, "A white person who is requested to pray for rain" in place of "by whose face rain is sought."[44]
Ibn Hajar said:

The clearest example of this type of *istisqa* is what Bayhaqi narrated in the *Dalail al-nubuwwa* (6:141)[45] from Muslim al-Malai from Anas who said that a bedouin went to the Prophet (ﷺ) and said, "O Messenger of Allah, we came to you at a time when our camels and our children are suffering. Then he recited poetry:
We have come to you when even our pregnant mothers' milk is dry, and the mother worries for her own life over her child's,
The child lets down his arms sitting still
For hunger, a hunger unstilled and uninterrupted.
We have nothing left from what our people eat
Except bitter colocynth and camel-wool mixed with
    blood.
And we have none but you to flee to, for where can
    people flee except to the Messengers?"
Then the Prophet (ﷺ) stood up and he was dragging his garment, and he climbed up the pulpit and said, "O Allah, send us water . . ." whereupon rain fell abundantly. Then the Prophet (ﷺ) said, "If Abu Talib were alive he would have liked to see this. Who will

44 Bukhari, *Sahih*, trans. Muhammad Muhsin Khan, 2:65.
45 Also Ibn Kathir, *al-Bidaya wal-nihaya* (6:90-91).

recite for us what he said?" Hearing this, Ali stood up
and said, "O Messenger of Allah, I think you mean his
saying:
>   A fair-skinned one by whose face rainclouds are
>   sought,
>   A caretaker for the orphans and protector of widows.
>   With him the clan of Hashim seek refuge from
>   calamities,
>   For they possess in him immense favor and
>   grace."46

2.8. BILAL'S PRAYER FOR RAIN AT THE PROPHET'S GRAVE

Al-Bayhaqi relates with a sound (*sahih*) chain:

> It is related from Malik al-Dar, Umar's treasurer,
> that the people suffered a drought during the succes-
> sorship of Umar, whereupon a man came to the grave
> of the Prophet (鋤) and said, "O Messenger of Allah,
> ask for rain for your Community, for verily they have
> but perished," after which the Prophet (鋤) appeared
> to him in a dream and told him, "Go to Umar and give
> him my greeting, then tell him that they will be
> watered. Tell him, You must be clever, you must be
> clever!" The man went and told Umar. The latter said,
> "O my Lord, I spare no effort except in what escapes
> my power!"

Ibn Kathir cites it thus from Bayhaqi and says, *isnaduhu
sahih*; Ibn Abi Shayba cites it in his *Musannaf* with a sound
(*sahih*) chain as confirmed by Ibn Hajar who says, *rawa Ibn Abi
Shayba bi isnadin sahih*, and cites the hadith in *Fath al-bari*.47
He identifies Malik al-Dar as Umar's treasurer (*khazin umar*)
and says that the man who visited and saw the Prophet (鋤) in
his dream is identified as the Companion Bilal ibn al-Harith,
and he counts this hadith among the reasons for Bukhari's
naming of the chapter "The people's request to their leader for
rain if they suffer drought." He also mentions it in *al-Isaba*,
where he says that Ibn Abi Khaythama cited it. This hadith is

---

46 Ibn Hajar, Ch. on "The People's Request of the Imam for *istisqa* in time of
drought in the book of *Istisaqa* in *Fath al-bari* (1989 ed. 2:629).

47 Ibn Hajar, *Fath al-bari*, Book of *istisqa* Ch. 3 (Beirut: Dar al-kutub al-ilmiyya,
1410/1989) 2:629-630.

discussed again further below with respect to Albani's claim, "We do not accept that this story is authentic . . ."

The legal inference here is not from the dream, because although the dream of seeing the Prophet (ﷺ) is truthful, a dream cannot be used to establish a ruling (*hukm*) due to the possibility that the person who saw it may make an error in its wording. Rather, the inference from this hadith is based on the action of the Companion Bilal ibn al-Harith. The fact that Bilal came to the grave of the Prophet (ﷺ), called out to him, and asked him to ask for rain is a proof that these actions are permitted. These actions fall under the rubric of asking the Prophet (ﷺ) for help (*istighatha*), seeking him as a means (*tawassul*), and using his intermediary (*tashaffu*). Since none of the Companions reprimanded him, it was understood that such actions are among the greatest acts of drawing near to Allah.

Yet in his edition of Ibn Hajar, the "Salafi" scholar Bin Baz rejects the hadith as a valid source for seeking rain through the Prophet (ﷺ), and brazenly condemns the act of the Companion who came to the grave, calling it *munkar* (aberrant) and *wasila ila al-shirk* (a means to associating partners to Allah).[48]

2.9. THE PROPHET SEES THE ACTIVITY OF HIS COMMUNITY

> The Prophet (ﷺ) said, "My life is a great good for you: you will relate about me and it will be related to you; and my death is a great good for you: your actions will be presented to me (in my grave) and if I see goodness I will praise Allah, and if see other than that I will ask forgiveness of Him for you."

Haythami says, "Al-Bazzar relates it and its sub-narrators are all men of sound hadith."[49] Qadi Iyad cites it[50] and Suyuti said, "Ibn Abi Usama cites it in his *Musnad* from the hadith of Bakr ibn Abd Allah al-Muzani, and al-Bazzar from the hadith

---

48 Haythami, *Majma al-zawaid* (9:24 #91).

49 Qadi Iyad, *al-Shifa* (1:56 of the Amman edition).

50 Al-Bazzar, *Manahil al-safa fi takhrij ahadith al-shifa* (Beirut 1988/1408) p. 31 (#8). He says the same in *al-Khasais al-kubra*.

of Ibn Masud with a sound (*sahih*) chain."[51] It is confirmed by al-Khafagi's and al-Qari's respective commentaries on *al-Shifa*. Al-Iraqi said, "Its chain is good" (*isnaduhu jayyid*).

The same hadith is cited in Shaykh al-Islam al-Taqi al-Subki's *Shifa al-siqam fi ziyarat khayr al-anam* (The healing of the sick concerning the visit of the best of creation), where he mentions that Bakr ibn Abd Allah al-Muzani reported it, and Ibn al-Jawzi mentions it through Bakr and then again through Anas ibn Malik in the penultimate chapter of the penultimate section of *al-Wafa*, both *huffaz* without giving the *isnad*. However, Ibn al-Jawzi specifies in the introduction of his book that he only included sound traditions in it. He also mentions the version through Aws ibn Aws, "The actions of human beings are shown to me every Thursday night preceding Friday."[52]

The former Grand Mufti of Egypt, Shaykh Hasanayn Muhammad Makhluf, wrote:

> The hadith means that the Prophet (ﷺ) is a great good for his Community during his life, because Allah the Exalted has preserved the Community through the secret of the Prophet's presence from misguidance and confusion and disagreement, and He has guided the people through the Prophet (ﷺ) to the manifest truth; and that after Allah took back the Prophet (ﷺ), our connection to the latter's goodness continues uncut and the extension of his goodness endures, over-shadowing us. The deeds of the Community are shown to him every day, and he glorifies Allah for the goodness that he finds, while he asks for His forgiveness for the small sins, and the alleviation of His punishment for the grave ones: and this is a tremendous good for us. There is therefore "goodness for the Community in his life, and in his death, goodness for the Community."
>
> Moreover, as has been established in the hadith, the Prophet (ﷺ) is alive in his grave with a special "isthmus-life" (*hayat barzakhiyya khassa*) stronger than the lives of the martyrs which the Quran spoke about in more than one verse. The nature of these two kinds of life cannot be known except by their

---

51 Al-Iraqi, *Tarh al-tathrib*.

52 See also *Fath al-bari* 10:415 and 11:385, al-Mundhiri's *al-Targhib wal-tarhib* 3:343 and *Musnad Ahmad* 4:484.

Bestower, the Glorious, the Exalted. He is able to do all things. His showing the Community's deeds to the Prophet (ﷺ) as an honorific gift for him and his Community is entirely possible rationally, and documented in the reports. There is no leeway for its denial; and Allah guides to His light whomever He pleases; and Allah knows best.[53]

2.10. AL-UTBI'S ACCOUNT AND OTHER EXAMPLES OF *TAWASSUL* AT THE PROPHET'S GRAVE

More hadith on *tawassul*:

Al-Utbi said, "As I was sitting by the grave of the Prophet (ﷺ), a Bedouin Arab came and said, "Peace be upon you, O Messenger of Allah! I have heard Allah saying, *"If they had only, when they were unjust to themselves, come unto thee and asked Allah's forgiveness, and the Messenger had asked forgiveness for them, they would have found Allah indeed Oft-Returning, Most Merciful"* (4:64), so I have come to you asking forgiveness for my sin, seeking your intercession with my Lord. Then he began to recite poetry:
O best of those whose bones are buried in the deep earth,
And from whose fragrance the depth and the height have become sweet,
May I be the ransom for a grave which thou inhabit,
And in which are found purity, bounty and munificence!
Then he left, and I dozed and saw the Prophet (ﷺ) in my sleep. He said to me, O Utbi, run after the Bedouin and give him glad tidings that Allah has forgiven him."

53 Shaykh Hasanayn Muhammad Makhluf, *Fatawa shariyya* (Cairo: Dar al-itisam, 1405/1985, 1:91-92).

The report is *mashhur* (well-known) and related by Nawawi,[54] Ibn Jamaa,[55] Ibn Aqil,[56] Ibn Qudama,[57] al-Qurtubi,[58] Samhudi,[59] Dahlan,[60] Ibn Kathir,[61] Abu al-Faraj ibn Qudama,[62] al-Bahuti al-Hanbali,[63] Taqi al-Din al-Subki,[64] Ibn al-Jawzi,[65] al-Bayhaqi,[66] Ibn Asakir,[67] Ibn Hajar al-Haytami,[68] Ibn al-Najjar.[69] A similar report is cited through Sufyan ibn Uyayna (Shafii's shaykh), and through Abu Said al-Samani on the authority of Ali.

Clearly, al-Utbi's account of the Arab's *tawassul* for forgiveness at the Prophet's grave is documented many times by scholars of the major schools in books dealing with *ziyara* (visiting the Prophet's grave in Madina) or *manasik* (rites of pilgrimage). In none of these books have the scholars rejected the hadith or called it weak.[70] Some contemporary "Salafi" scholars choose to contest this grade of *mashhur*, but these are not as reliable as the sources named above. Little or no weight should be given to the "Salafis" recourse to the isolated opinions of Ibn Taymiyya or Ibn Abd al-Hadi, who have cast aspersions on the authenticity of the report, (in the words of Ibn Jamaa).

The sources also relate the report of Ibn Abi Fudayk, one of the early scholars of Madina and one of Shafii's shaykhs, who said:

> I heard one of the authorities whom I have met say, "It has reached us that whoever stands at the Prophet's grave and recites, *"Allah and His angels*

---

54 Nawawi, *Adhkar*, Makka ed. p. 253-254, *al-Majmu* 8:217, and *al-Idah fi man-asik al-hajj*, chapters on visiting the grave of the Prophet.
55 Ibn Jamaa, *Hidayat al-salik* 3:1384.
56 Ibn Aqil, *al-Tadhkira*.
57 Ibn Qudama, *al-Mughni* 3:556-4557.
58 Al-Qurtubi, *Tafsir* of 4:64 in *Ahkam al-quran* 5:265.
59 Samhudi, *Khulasat al-wafa* p. 121 (from Nawawi).
60 Dahlan, *Khulasat al-kalam* 2:247.
61 Ibn Kathir, *Tafsir* 2:306, and *al-Bidayat wal-nihayat* 1:180.
62 Abu al-Faraj ibn Qudama, *al-Sharh al-kabir* 3:495.
63 Al-Bahuti, *Kashshaf al-qina* 5:30.
64 Taqi al-Din al-Subki, *Shifa al-siqam* p. 52.
65 Ibn al-Jawzi, *Muthir al-gharam al-sakin ila ashraf al-amakin* p. 490.
66 Al-Bayhaqi, *Shuab al-iman* #4178.
67 Ibn Asakir, *Mukhtasar tarikh dimashq* 2:408.
68 Ibn Hajar al-Haytami, *al-Jawhar al-munazzam* [commentary on Nawawi's *Idah*].
69 Ibn al-Najjar, *Akhbar al-madina* p. 147.
70 See, for example, the translations of Ibn al-Jawzi, Nawawi, and Ibn Jamma in the last section of this book.

send blessings on the Prophet . . ." (33:56) and then says, "May Allah bless you, O Muhammad" (*sallallahu alayka ya Muhammad*) seventy times, an angel will call him saying, 'May Allah bless you, O so-and-so; none of your needs will be left unfulfilled.'"[71]

The *muhaddith* al-Samhudi and others also relate the account of the Arab who sought the Prophet's means at his grave:

> Al-Asmai said, I saw a Bedouin stand at the Prophet's grave and say, "O Allah, here is Your Beloved, and I am Your servant, and Satan is Your enemy. If You forgive me, Your Beloved will be happy, Your servant will attain victory, and Your enemy will be angry. If You do not forgive me, Your Beloved will be sad, Your enemy will be satisfied, and Your servant will be destroyed. But You are more noble, O my Lord, than to allow Your Beloved to be sad, Your enemy to be satisfied, and Your servant to be destroyed. O Allah, the highborn Arabs, if one of their leaders die, release one of their slaves over his grave in his honor, and this is the leader of the worlds: therefore release me over his grave, O Most Merciful of the merciful!" Al-Asmai said, "I said to him, "O brother of the Arabs! Allah has surely forgiven you and released you for the beauty of this request."[72]

Al-Hafiz Ibn al-Jawzi:[73]

> (*Al-hafiz*) Abu Bakr al-Minqari said, I was with (*al-hafiz*) al-Tabarani and (*al-hafiz*) Abu al-Shaykh (Abd Allah ibn Muhammad al-Asbahani) in the Prophet's Mosque, in some difficulty. We became very hungry. That day and the next we didn't eat. When it was time for the night prescribed prayer (*isha*), I went to the Prophet's grave and said, "O Messenger of Allah, we are hungry, we are hungry" (*ya rasullallah al-ju al-ju*)! Then I left. Abu al-Shaykh said to me, "Sit. Either there will be food for us, or death.' I slept

---

71 Ibn Jamma related it in *Hidayat al-salik* 3:1382-1383, Ibn al-Jawzi in *Muthir al-gharam* p. 487, Qadi Iyad in *al-Shifa* and Bayhaqi in *Shuab al-iman* (#4169).
72 Narrated by al-Samhudi in *Khulast al-wafa* (Madina, 1972) p. 123 by Shaykh al-Islam Ibn Hajar al-Haytami in his *Jawahir al-munazzam* (Cairo: Dar jawami al-kalim, 1992) p. 126-127, and others.
73 Ibn al-Jawzi, *Kitab al-wafa* (p. 818 #1536).

and Abu al-Shaykh slept. Al-Tabarani stayed awake, researching something. Then an Alawi (a descendant of Ali) came knocking at the door with two boys, each one carrying a palm-leaf basket filled with food. We sat up and ate. We thought that the children would take back the remainder but they left everything behind. When we finished, the Alawi said, 'O people, did you complain to the Prophet (ﷺ)? I saw him in my sleep and he ordered me to bring something to you.'

Imam Bukhari said that he wrote his biographical book on the subnarrators of authentic hadith *al-Tarikh al-kabir* by the Prophet's graveside, under the light of the moon.[74]

Musnad Ahmad, Imam Ahmad's compilation of 30,000 mostly sound narrations from the Prophet (ﷺ), was held in such high reverence that it was read in the sixth century by a society of devout hadith scholars from cover to cover in fifty-six sittings before the grave of the Prophet (ﷺ) in Madina.[75] Where is such devotion to the Prophet (ﷺ) found today?

Ibn Hajar said in Sulayman ibn Sunayd ibn Nashwan's biographical notice in his *al-Durar al-kamina* that he performed forty pilgrimages. On the fortieth he was seized by fatigue and fell asleep by the side of the Noble Grave. Thereupon he saw the Prophet (ﷺ) who told him, "O So-and-so, how many times have you come, and you have received nothing from me? Give me your hand." He gave him his hand, and the Prophet (ﷺ) wrote on it an invocation against fever that, if ever he suffered from fever, would cure him by Allah's permission. This invocation is, "I have sought refuge with a Master who never judges unjustly nor leads to other than victory. Go out, O fever, from this body, nor does pain of any sort follow this."[76]

---

74 It is related by Ibn al-Jawzi in *Sifat al-safwa* (4:147) and al-Subki in *Tabaqat al-shafiyya al-kubra* (2:216).

75 Muhammad Zubayr Siddiqi, *Hadith Literature: Its Origin, Development and Special Features* (Islamic Texts Society, 1993) p. 51.

76 Ajluni mentions it in *Kashf al-khafa* (#1175).

3. SEEKING MEANS OF APPROACH (*TAWASSUL*) TO ALLAH THROUGH SAINTS

The evidence for seeking ways of nearness to Allah (*tawassul*) through the saints is also abundant. It suffices that Allah strictly warns all believers to keep company with them when He says, *"O believers! Be wary of Allah, and keep company with the truthful!"* (9:119). He enjoins us to follow those who have turned to Him in true and complete repentance (31:15). The Prophet (ﷺ) said to al-Firasi, about asking from people, "If you absolutely must ask from people, then ask from the righteous ones" (*in kunta la budda sailan fasal al-salihin*).[1] There is no doubt that the visit of pious persons for *tawassul* is a *sunna* in Islam.[2]

Some people think that if a supplication from a holy man is answered while he is alive, he cannot help you if he is dead, as though the holy man, or shaykh, or saint, is the origin of that help. On the contrary, it is always Allah who is the source of the *baraka* and never a human being. So to think that Allah gives only when the saint is alive, and that when he is dead, Allah does not give anymore, is to say that the source is the person and not Allah in the first place! In reality, it is Allah who is giving help in both cases: life and death.

Some "Salafis" object to seeking blessings from saints after their death. These objections are based on the false belief that Allah's influence through the saints requires the saint to be

---

1 Narrated by Ahmad in the *Musnad*, Abu Dawud, and al-Nasai in their *Sunan*. Al-Dhahabi said, "Its chain is good (*isnaduhu salih*)." See Shahabi, *Mujam al-shuyukh* (Taif: Maktabat al-siddiq, 1408/1988) 2:420 (#1028).

2 This is supported by the chapters to that effect entitled *Bab ziyarat al-salihin* in the books of etiquette and invocations.

alive. As mentioned earlier, Allah's gift to the saints is independent of their being alive or dead, since in both cases the real
power belongs to Allah, and the saints are only secondary
means with no effective power in themselves. Moreover, the
views of the early and late Imams and scholars quoted below
also confirm that the "Salafis" objections to *tawassul* through
the saints after their death do not withstand scrutiny.

It is part of the Muslim belief that *abdal*, or substitutes-
saints, exist–so called because, as the Prophet (鷺) said, "None
of them dies except Allah substitutes another in his place,"–
and that they are among the religious leaders of the
Community.[3] None other than Ibn Taymiyya writes at the end
of his *Aqida wasitiyya*:

> The true adherents of Islam in its pristine purity
> are the Sunnis. In their ranks the truthful saints (*sid-
> diqin*), the martyrs, and the righteous are to be found.
> Among them are the great men of guidance and illu-
> mination, of recorded integrity and celebrated virtue.
> The Substitutes (*abdal*) and the Imams of religion are
> to be found among them and the Muslims are in full
> accord concerning their guidance. These are the
> Victorious Group about whom the Prophet (鷺) said,
> "A group within my Community manifestly continues
> to be in the truth. Neither those who oppose them nor
> those who abandon them can do them harm, from now
> on until the Day of Resurrection."[4]

The Prophet (鷺) emphasized in many authentic narrations
the benefits brought to all creation through the intercession of
Allah's saints and their standing with Him. Suyuti provided
many examples of this type of universal intercession, including
the following:[5]

1. Imam Ahmad ibn Hanbal narrates:

> . . . The people of Sham were mentioned in front
> of Ali ibn Abi Talib while he was in Iraq, and they
> said, "Curse them, O Commander of the Believers."
> He replied, "No, I heard the Messenger of Allah say,

---

3 See #3 below.
4 Ibn Taymiyya, *Aqida wasitiyya* (Salafiyya edition) p. 36.
5 Suyuti in his *fatwa* on the *abdal* in his *Hawi li al-fatawi*.

'The Substitutes (al-abdal) are in Sham and they are forty men, every time one of them dies, Allah substitutes another in his place. By means of them Allah brings down the rain, gives (Muslims) victory over their enemies, and averts punishment from the people of Sham.'"[6]

Al-Haythami said, "The men in its chains are all those of the *sahih* except for Sharih ibn Ubayd, and he is trustworthy (*thiqa*)." Sakhawi mentions this narration in his *Maqasid* and agrees.[7] However, he is of the opinion that it is more likely a saying of Ali himself.

2. Al-Hakim narrated the following and graded it sound (*sahih*). Al-Dhahabi confirmed him:

Ali said: "Do not curse the people of Sham, for among them are the Substitutes (al-abdal), but curse their injustice."

The above is a narration of Ali not attributed to the Prophet (ﷺ). Note, however, that any religious knowledge unattainable through *ijtihad* and authentically conveyed from one of the Companions is considered a hadith by the experts of that science.

3. Tabarani said in his *Mujam al-awsat*:

Anas said that the Prophet (ﷺ) said, "The earth will never lack forty men similar to the Friend of the Merciful [Prophet Abraham (ﷺ)], and through them people receive rain and are given help. None of them dies except Allah substitutes another in his place." Qatada said, "We do not doubt that al-Hasan [al-Basri] is one of them."

Ibn Hibban narrates it through Abu Hurayra as, "The earth will never lack forty men similar to Abraham the Friend of the Merciful, and through them you are helped, receive your sustenance, and receive rain."[8]

4. Imam Ahmad also narrated through Abd al-Wahhab ibn Ata:

6 Ahmad Ibn Hanbal, *Musnad* (1:112).
7 Sakhawi, *Maqasid* (p. 33 #8).
8 Ibn Hibban, *al-Tarikh*.

The Prophet (ﷺ) said, "The Substitutes in this Community are thirty like Abraham, the Friend of the Merciful. Every time one of them dies, Allah substitutes another one in his place." Ahmad said, "Other than this is also narrated from Abd al-Wahhab, but it is denounced (*munkar*)."[9]

5. Abu Dawud through three different good chains, Imam Ahmad, Ibn Abi Shayba, Abu Yala, al-Hakim, and Bayhaqi narrated:

Umm Salama, the wife of the Prophet (ﷺ), said, "Disagreement will occur at the death of a Caliph and a man of the people of Madina will come forth flying to Makka. Some of the people of Makka will come to him, bring him out against his will and swear allegiance to him between the Corner and the *maqam*. An expeditionary force will then be sent against him from Sham but will be swallowed up in the desert between Makka and Madina, and when the people see that, the Substitutes (*abdal*) of Sham and the best people (*asaba*) of Iraq will come to him and swear allegiance to him . . ."[10]

6. Imam Ahmad, Ibn Abi al-Dunya, Abu Nuaym, Bayhaqi, and Ibn Asakir narrate from Julays:

Wahb ibn Munabbih said: I saw the Prophet (ﷺ) in my sleep, so I said, "*Ya Rasul Allah*, where are the Substitutes (*budala*) of your Community?" He gestured with his hand towards Sham. I asked, "*Ya Rasul Allah*, aren't there any in Iraq?" He said, "Yes, Muhammad ibn Wasi, Hassan ibn Abi Sinan, and Malik ibn Dinar, who walks among the people similarly to Abu Dharr in his time."[11]

7. Nawawi mentions that the hadith master Hammad ibn Salama ibn Dinar (d. 167) was considered to be one of the

---

9 Imam Ahmad in the *Musnad* (5:322). Hakim Tirmidhi cites it in *Nawadir al-usul* and Ahmad's student al-Khallal in his *Karamat al-awliya*. Haythami said its men are those of the *sahih* except Abd al-Wahid who was declared trustworthy by al-Ijli and Abu Zara (as well as Yahya ibn Main). He is one of the narrators of Imam Muslim and also Tirmidhi.

10 Abu Dawud, *Sunan*, English #4273, Imam Ahmad *Musnad* 6:316, Ibn Abi Shayba *Musannaf*.

11 Imam Ahmad, *Kitab al-zuhd*.

abdal. Sakhawi in his notice on the narrations of the *abdal* already referred to said:

> What makes this hadith stronger and indicates its currency among the Imams is the statement of our Imam, al-Shafii, concerning a certain man: "We considered him one of the *abdal*," and Bukhari's statement concerning another: "They did not doubt that he was one of the *abdal*," and other than these two among the highly meticulous scholars, hadith masters, and imams [such as Qatada, see above] also used this description for other people, stating that they were of the *abdal*.[12]

It is extremely telling that in their derogatory references to the *abdal*, the "Salafis" never mention the strong reports from the scholars listed above, but mention only the weakest reports they can find, neglecting what is established as authentic.[13] They contradict their own imam, Ibn Taymiyya, and his assertion that "the Substitutes (*abdal*) and the Imams of religion are to be found among them [the true adherents of Islam in its pristine purity], and the Muslims are in full accord concerning their guidance."[14]

The hadiths of the *abdal* of Sham are confirmed by the very high status of Sham in the hadiths of the Prophet's Night Journey (*isra* and *miraj*). The Prophet (ﷺ) called Sham the purest of Allah's lands; the place where religion, belief, and safety are found in times of dissension, and the home of the saints for whose sake Allah sends sustenance to believers and victory over their enemies.

8. Ibn Asakir relates from Ibn Masud that the Prophet (ﷺ) compared the world to a little rain water on a mountain plateau from which the clear water (*safw*) had already been drunk and from which only the *kadar* or dregs remained.[15] Al-Huwjiri and al-Qushayri mention it in their chapters on *tasawwuf*.[16] Ibn al-Athir defines *safw* and *safwa* as "the best of any matter, its quintessence, and purest part."[17] The quintes-

---

12 Nawawi, *Bustan al-arifin*, Sakhawi, 198 ed. p. 31.
13 Such as 1, 2, 4, 5, and 7 above.14 Nawawi, *Aqida wasitiyya.*
15 Ibn Asakir in *Tahdhib tarikh dimashq al-kabir.*
16 Al-Hujwiri, *Kashf al-mahjub* and al-Qushayri, *al-Risala al-Qushayriyya.*
17 Ibn al-Athir in his dictionary *al-Nihaya.*

sence spoken of by the Prophet (ﷺ) is Sham, because he called Sham "the quintessence of Allah's lands" (safwat Allah min biladih).[18]

9. Abu al-Darda narrated that the Prophet (ﷺ) said:

> As I was sleeping I saw the Column of the Book being carried away from under my head. I feared lest it would be taken away, so I followed it with my eyes and saw that it was being planted in Sham. Verily, belief in the time of dissensions will be in Sham.

Haythami said that Ahmad reported it according to a chain whose narrators are all men of the sahih, or sound narrations, and that al-Bazzar narrated it with a chain whose narrators are the men of sound hadith except for Muhammad ibn Amir al-Antaki, and he is thiqa, or trustworthy.

In the version Tabarani narrated from Ibn Amr, the Prophet (ﷺ) repeats three times, "When the dissensions take place, belief will be in Sham."[19] One manuscript reads, "Safety will be in Sham." Al-Haythami said the men in its chain are those of sound hadith except for Ibn Lahia, and he is fair (hasan).

10. Al-Tabarani relates from Abd Allah ibn Hawala that the Prophet (ﷺ) said:

> I saw on the night that I was enraptured a white column resembling a pearl, which the angels were carrying. I said to them, "What are you carrying?" They replied, "The Column of the Book. We have been ordered to place it in Sham." Later, in my sleep, I saw that the Column of the Book was snatched away from under my headrest (wisadati). I began to fear lest Allah the Almighty had abandoned the people of the earth. My eyes followed where it went. It was a brilliant light in front of me. Then I saw it was placed in Sham." Abd Allah ibn Hawala said, "O Messenger of Allah, choose for me (where I should go)." The Prophet (ﷺ) said, alayka bi al-sham–"You must go to Sham."[20]

18 Tabarani related it from Irbad ibn Sariya and Haythami authenticated the chain of transmission in his book Majma al-zawaid, chapter entitled Bab fadail al-sham.

19. Tabarani, Mujam al-kabir and al-Mujam al-awsat.

20 Al-hafiz al-Haythami said in Majma al-zawaid: "The narrators in its chain of transmission are all those of sound hadith except Salih ibn Rustum and he is thiqa—trustworthy.

Shaykh Abd al-Qadir Jilani said:

And he said (may Allah be pleased with him):
When the servant of Allah is in a trial, he first tries to
escape from it with his own efforts, and when he fails,
in this he seeks the help of others from among men
such as the kings and men of authority, people of the
world, men of wealth, and in the case of illness and
physical suffering, from physicians and doctors; but if
the escape is not secured by these he then turns
towards his Creator and Lord the Great and Mighty
and applies to Him with prayer and humility and
praise.

So long as he finds the resources in his own self
he does not turn towards the people and so long as he
finds resources in the people he does not turn towards
the Creator. Further, when he does not get any help
from Allah he throws himself in His presence and continues in this state, begging and praying humbly
entreating and praising and submitting his neediness
in fear and hope. Allah, however, tires him out in his
prayer and does not accept it until he is completely
disappointed in all the means of the world. The decree
of Allah and His work then manifest themselves
through him and this servant of Allah passes away
from all the worldly means and the activities and
efforts of the world and retains just his soul.

At this stage he sees nothing but the work of
Allah and becomes, of necessity, a believer in the
unity of Allah (*tawhid*) to the degree of certainty, that
in reality there is no doer of anything excepting Allah
and no mover and stopper excepting Him and no good
and no evil and no loss and no gain and no benefit and
no conferring and no withholding and no opening and
no closing and no death and no life and no honor and
no dishonor and no affluence and no poverty but in
the hand of Allah.

He then becomes in the presence of Allah as a
nursing baby in the hands of its nurse and a dead
corpse in the hands of the person who gives it the
funeral bath and a ball is before the stick of the polo-
player, as it keeps revolving and rolling and changing
position after position and condition after condition,

and he feels no strength either in his own self or in others besides himself for any movement. He thus vanishes from his own self out into the work of his Master.

So he sees nothing but his Master and His work, and hears nothing and understands nothing excepting Him. If he sees anything it is His work and if he hears and knows anything, he hears His word and knows through His knowledge and he becomes gifted with His gifts and becomes lucky through His nearness and through His nearness he becomes decorated and honored and becomes pleased and comforted and satisfied with His promise and is drawn towards His word and he feels aversion for and is repelled from those besides Him and he desires and relies on His remembrance and he becomes established in Him, the Great and Mighty, and relies on Him and obtains guidance from, and clothes and dresses himself with, the light of His knowledge and is apprised of the rare points of His knowledge and of the secrets of His power and he hears and remembers only from Him the Great, the Mighty, and then offers thanks and praise therefore and takes to prayer.[21]

Imam Ibn Hajar al-Haytami said:

When Imam al-Shafii was in Baghdad, he would visit the grave of Imam Abu Hanifa, give him *salam*, and then ask Allah for the fulfillment of his need through his means (*yatawassal ilallah taala bihi fi qada hajatihi*).[22]

Imam Kawthari mentioned that the *hafiz* al-Khatib al-

---

21 Abd al-Qadir Jilani, in the Third Discourse of his masterpiece *Futuh al-ghayb*, as adapted slightly from the 1958 translation of M. Aftab-ud-Din Ahmad published in Lahore.

22 Al-Haytami, *al-Khayrat al-hisan* (Cairo: al-Halabi, n.d.) p. 63. It is also related that Imam Ahmad made *tawassul* through Imam Shafii to the point that his son, Abd Allah, expressed his surprise and Ahmad replied, "Al-Shafii is like the sun for the people and like health for the body." When Imam Shaffi heard that the people of al-Maghrib made *tawassul* to Allah through Imam Malik, he did not object to it.

Baghdadi mentions Shafii's *tawassul* through Abu Hanifa with a good chain.[23]
Haytami also said in many places in his books:[24]

> Imam Shafii made *tawassul* through the Family of the Prophet (𝕄) (*Ahl al-Bayt*) when he said: The Family of the Prophet (𝕄) are my means and my intermediary to him. Through them I hope to be given my record with the right hand tomorrow (*al al-nabi dhariati wa hum ilayhi wasilati arju bihim uta ghadan bi yadi al-yamini sahifati*).[25]

The *hafiz* al-Iraqi relates with his chain:

> We narrated that the Imam Ahmad sought blessing from drinking the washing-water of Imam al-Shafii's shirt, and Ibn Taymiyya himself also related it.[26]

Al-Khatib relates that the *hafiz* Abu Nuaym considered it incumbent upon all Muslims to invoke Allah for Abu Hanifa in their prayer due to his preservation of the Prophet's *sunan* and *fiqh* for them.[27] This is explained by the fact that among Abu Hanifa's outstanding merits is his standing as the first in Islam to have compiled a book of jurisprudence (*fiqh*).[28]

Al-hafiz Abu Ali al-Ghassani relates:

> Abu al-Fath Nasr ibn al-Hasan al-Sakani al-Samarqandi came to us in 464 and said, We had a drought in Samarqand some years ago. The people made the *istisqa* prayer (prayer for rain) but they did not get rain. A saintly man named al-Salah came to the judge and said to him, "I have an opinion I would like to show you. My opinion is that you come out followed by the people and that you all go to the grave of

---

23 Imam Kawthari, *Maqalat* (p. 412) and al-Baghdadi in the beginning of his *Tarikh Baghdad* (1:123).

24 Haythami, *al-Sawaiq al-muhriqa li ahl al-dalal wal-zandaqa* (cf. p. 180) and *al-Khayrat al-hisan* (p. 69).

25 This is also found in *Diwan al-Shafii* as edited by Umar Faruq al-Dabbagh (Beirut: Dar al-arqam, n.d.) p. 50.

26 Al-Iraqi, *Fath al-mutaal*.

27 Al-Khatib al-Baghdadi, *Tarikh Baghdad* 13:344.

28 Suyuti, *Tabyid al-sahifa* (1413/1992 ed.) p. 161.

Imam Muhammad ibn Ismail al-Bukhari and make *istisqa* there. Perhaps Allah will give us rain." The judge said, "What a good opinion you have." He came out and the people followed him, and he prayed for rain in front of them at the grave while people wept and sought the intercession of the one who was in it. Allah sent such heavy rain that those who were in Khartenk (where this took place, 3 miles away from Samarqand) could not reach Samarqand for seven days because of the rain's abundance.[29]

The late *mufti* of Lebanon al-Shahid al-Shaykh Hasan Khalid said:

> *Tawassul* was declared permissible in our own time by the *mufti* of the world, our shaykh the savant Abu al-Yusr Abidin. We went with him to Nawa, a place in Hawran wherein is buried the Shaykh Muhyiddin al-Nawawi. When we arrived at his grave, our Shaykh Abu al-Yusr ordered us to ask Allah the Exalted for our need in front of him and said to us, "The *dua* (invocation) at his grave is answered."[30]

Ibn al-Jawzi, in his biographies of the saints entitled *Sifat al-safwa*, lists many of those at whose graves *tabarruk* (seeking blessing) and *tawassul* is recommended. Among them are:

> Abu Ayyub al-Ansari: "Al-Waqidi said, It has reached us that the Eastern Romans visit his grave and seek rain through his intercession when they suffer from droughts." Mujahid said, "People would uncover the space above his grave and it would rain."[31]

> Maruf al-Karkhi (d. 200H): "His grave can be seen in Baghdad, and one seeks blessings with it. *Al-Hafiz* Ibrahim al-Harbi (d. 285H)–Imam Ahmad's companion–used to say, Maruf's grave is proven medicine."[32]

---

29 Ibn al-Subki, *Tabaqat al-shafiiyya* 2:234.

30 Al-Shahid al-Shaykh Hasan Khalid in his *fatwa* on *tawassul* on September 16, 1980 (reprinted in the Qaqf Ikhlas offset reprint of Sayyid Ahmad ibn Zayni Dahlan's book *Fitnat al-wahhabiyya* 1992).

31 Ibn al-Jawzi, *Sifat al-safwa* (1:243).

32 *Ibid*. (2:214).

Ibn al-Jawzi adds, "We ourselves go to Ibrahim al-Harbi's grave and seek blessings with it."[33]

Al-hafiz al-Dhahabi also relates Ibrahim al-Harbi's saying about Maruf al-Karkhi, "Maruf's grave is proven medicine."[34]

Abu al-Hasan al-Daraqutni said, "We used to seek blessings from Abu al-Fath al-Qawasi's grave."[35]

Abu al-Qasim al-Waiz: "His grave can be seen in Ahmad ibn Hanbal's cemetery and it is sought for blessings." Related in the notice on Abd al-Samad ibn Umar ibn Muhammad ibn Ishaq.[36]

Al-hafiz Abu al-Qasim Ibn Asakir says in *Musnad Abi Uwana* (1:430), "Abu Abd Allah Muhammad ibn Muham-mad ibn Umar al-Saffar said to me that the grave of Abu Uwana in Isfarayin [near Naishabur] is a place of visitation for the whole world (*mazar al-alam*) and a place for obtaining blessing for the entire creation (*mutabarrak al-khalq*)."

Al-Hafiz Diya al-Din al-Maqdisi al-Hanbali said that he heard the *hafiz* Abd al-Ghani al-Maqdisi al-Hanbali say that something like an abcess appeared on his upper arm for which there was found no medicine.[37] He came to Ahmad ibn Hanbal's grave and applied his arm against it, after which he found himself healed. Imam Kawthari said that he read this account in Diya al-Din's own handwriting.[38]

3.1. DO THOSE WHO HAVE LEFT THIS LIFE KNOW ABOUT THE AFFAIRS OF THE LIVING?

Ibn Qayyim narrates with his chain from Ibn al-Mubarak on the authority of Abu Ayyub al-Ansari that the latter said, "The works of the living are clear to the dead. Whenever they

---

33 *Ibid.* (2:410).

34 Al-Dhahabi, *Siyar alam al-nubala* (9:343).

35 *Ibid.* (2:471).

36 *Ibid* (2:482).

37 Al-Hafiz Diya al-Din al-Maqsidi al-Hanbali, *al-Hikayat al-manuthura* (Zahiriyya ms. 98, an autograph).

38 Kawthari, *Maqalat al-kawthari* (Riyadh and Beirut: Dar al-ahnaf, 1414/1993) p. 407, 412.

see a good deed they rejoice and are pleased; but if they see evil they say, O Allah, return its equivalent in good."[39]

Ibn Qayyim, and Ibn Abi al-Dunya narrated that Abbad ibn Abbad called upon Ibrahim ibn Salih while he was ruler of Palestine and said, "Exhort me." He said, "With what should I exhort you? May Allah set you right! I have heard that the works of the living are clear as day to their dead relatives. So consider what is laid open to the Messenger of Allah of your work." Ibrahim wept until his beard was wet.[40]

Imam Suyuti has an entire chapter devoted to that topic entitled, "The Exhibition of the deeds of the living to the dead."[41] In it he lists fifteen hadiths and sayings of the Companions:

> 1. Ahmad in his *Musnad*, al-Hakim al-Tirmidhi in *Nawadir al-usul*, and Ibn Mindah narrated from Anas that the Prophet (ﷺ) said, "Your deeds are shown to your relatives and ancestors among the dead. If they consist in good they are happy with it, if otherwise, they say, O Allah! Don't let them die before you guide them as you have guided us."
>
> 2. Al-Tayalisi in his *Musnad* narrated from Jabir ibn Abd Allah that the Prophet (ﷺ) said, "Your deeds are shown to your relatives and ancestors in their graves. If they consist in good they are happy with it, if otherwise, they say, O Allah! Inspire them to act in obedience to You."
>
> 3. Ibn al-Mubarak and Ibn Abi al-Dunya in *Kitab al-qubur* narrated from Abu Ayyub, "Your deeds are shown to the dead, who rejoice if they see any good in them, and if they see evil in them they say, O Allah, give them another opportunity."
>
> 4. Ibn Abi Shayba in his *Musannaf*, al-Hakim al-Tirmidhi, and Ibn Abi al-Dunya narrated from Ibrahim ibn Maysara that when Abu Ayyub campaigned to take Constantinople he passed by a story-teller who was saying, "What a servant does in the morning, before evening is shown to those in the hereafter who know him; and what he does at the end of the day is shown to them by the next morning." Abu Ayyub said, "Be careful what you say." He replied, "By

39 Ibn Qayyim, *Kitab al-ruh*.
40 *Ibid.* and Ibn Abi al-Dunya in *Kitab al-qubur*.
41 Suyuti, *Sharh al-sudur* (p. 263-266).

Allah it is as I said." Abu Ayyub said, "O Allah, I seek refuge in You lest You reveal my shame to Ubada ibn al-Samit and Sad ibn Ubada concerning what I did after them."

5. Al-Hakim al-Tirmidhi cited in *Nawadir al-usul* the hadith of Abd al-Ghafur ibn Abd al-Aziz from his father, from his grandfather, whereby the Prophet (ﷺ) said, "One's deeds are shown to Allah on Monday and Thursday, and they are shown to prophets as well as fathers and mothers on Fridays, at which time they rejoice for the good deeds, and the latter increase the brightness and light of their faces. Therefore be wary of Allah and do not harm your dead."

6. Al-Hakim al-Tirmidhi cited, as well as Ibn Abi al-Dunya[42] and Bayhaqi[43] from al-Numan ibn Bashir: I heard the Prophet (ﷺ) say, "Allah, Allah! [Be wary of Him] concerning your brethren among the dwellers of graves, for your deeds are shown to them."

7. Ibn Abi al-Dunya and al-Asbahani in *al-Targhib* cited from Abu Hurayra that the Prophet (ﷺ) said, "Do not shame your dead with your evil deeds for your deeds are shown to your relatives among the dwellers of the graves."

8. Ibn Abi al-Dunya, Ibn Mindah, and Ibn Asakir narrated from Ahmad ibn Abd Allah ibn Abi al-Hawari: My brother Muhammad ibn Abd Allah related to me, Abbad al-Khawass walked in to see Ibrahim ibn Salih al-Hashimi when the latter was governor of Palestine. Ibrahim said, "Admonish me." He replied, "It has reached me that the deeds of the living are shown to their relatives among the deceased. Therefore beware what is shown to Allah's Messenger from your deeds."

9. Ibn Abi al-Dunya cited from Abu al-Darda that he used to say, "O Allah, I seek refuge in You lest my maternal uncle Abd Allah ibn Rawaha should loathe me when I meet him."

10. Ibn al-Mubarak and al-Asbahani cited from Abu al-Darda that he said, "Your deeds are shown to the dead, whereupon they rejoice and they are saddened" and he would say, "O Allah, I seek refuge in You from committing a deed by which Abd Allah ibn Rawaha should be dishonored."

42 Al-Hakim al-Tirmidhi, *Book of Dreams (Kitab al-manamat)*.
43 Bayhaqi, *Shuab al-iman*.

This Abd Allah ibn Rawaha al-Ansari was the great-grandson of the poet Imru al-Qays and was himself a great poet among the Companions. He said of the Prophet (ﷺ):

> *Law lam takun fihi ayatun mubina lakana manzaruhu yunabbiuka bi al-khabari* (even if there were not, concerning him, clear and evident signs, yet the sight of him would have told you the news).

Ibn Hajar narrated it and said, "This is the most beautiful verse of poetry by which the Prophet (ﷺ) was ever praised."[44] Ibn Sayyid al-Nas said of Ibn Rawaha:

> He was killed as a martyr on the day of Muta in Jumada 8 before the conquest of Makka. On that day he was one of the commanders. He was one of the poets who did good and who used to ward Allah's Messenger from harm. It was concerning him and his two friends Hassan (ibn Thabit) and Kab (ibn Zuhayr) that was revealed the verse: "Except those who believe and do good deeds and remember Allah abundantly."

Hisham ibn Urwa narrated from his father that the latter said:

> I never saw anyone more aggressive or faster in his poetry than Abd Allah ibn Rawaha. I heard Allah's Messenger say to him one day, "Recite some poetry appropriate to the moment, while I look at you." He rose up then and there and said:

> *inni tafarrastu fika al-khayra arifuhu*
> *wallahu yalamu anna ma khanani al-basaru*
> *anta al-nabiyyu wa man yuhramu shafaatahu*
> *yawma al-hisabi laqad azra bihi al-qadaru*
> *fa thabbat allahu ma ataka min hasanin*
> *tathbita musa wa nasran kalladhi nusiru*
> I foresee for you immense good, of this I am certain.
> Allah knows that my sight never betrayed me.
> You are the Prophet (ﷺ), and whoever is deprived of your intercession

44 Ibn Hajar, *al-Isaba* (2:299).

On the Day of Reckoning, his destiny is disgrace.
May Allah make firm all the good that He gave
   you,
With a firmness like Moses' and the same victory.

Upon hearing this the Prophet (ﷺ) said to him, "And you also, may Allah make you firm, O Ibn Rawaha." Hisham ibn Urwa continued, Allah indeed made him firm with the staunchest firmness. He died as a martyr, and paradise was opened for him and he entered it. End of Ibn Sayyid al-Nas's words. Blessings and peace on the Prophet (ﷺ), his Family, and his Companions![45]

11. Ibn al-Mubarak also cited from Uthman ibn Abd Allah ibn Aws that Said ibn al-Jubayr said to him, "Give me permission to see my brother's daughter"–Uthman's wife and the daughter of Amr ibn Aws–so he permitted him. He went and asked her, "How is your husband treating you?" She said, "He does his utmost with me." Then Said said, "O Uthman! Treat her well, for there is nothing that you do with her except its news reaches Amr ibn Aws." Uthman said, "The news of the living reaches the dead?" He said, "Yes, there is no one with an intimate friend [among the deceased] except the news of his relatives reaches him. If it is good he rejoices and is cheered by it, and if it is bad he is saddened and distraught."

12. Ibn Abi al-Dunya cited the following report through Abu Bakr ibn Iyash, from a grave-digger who was with the Banu Asad and who said, I was among the graves one night when I heard someone in a grave say, "O Abu Abd Allah!" and another answered, "What, O Jabir?" He said, "Tomorrow our mother will be coming to us." The other replied, "Of what use will that be for her? Let her not come, for my father became angry with her and swore that he would not pray over her." The next day a man came to me and said, "Dig a grave for me between these two," indicating the graves from where I had heard the voices coming. Whereupon I said, "This one's name is Jabir, and that one is Abd Allah?" He said, "Yes!" So I told him

---

45 Ibn Sayyid al-Nas, *Minah al-madh* p. 166 and The Poets 26:227.

what I had heard. Then the man said, "Yes, I had sworn that I would not pray over her, but I shall break my oath and pray over her."

13. Abu Nuaym cited from Ibn Masud that the latter said, "Keep relations with those your father kept relations with, for that is the way relations are kept on behalf of the dead in their graves."

14. Ibn Hibban cited from Ibn Umar that the Prophet (ﷺ) said, "Whoever likes to keep relations with his father in his grave, let him keep relations with his father's brothers after him."

15. Abu Dawud and Ibn Hibban cited from Abu Usayd al-Saidi that a man came to the Prophet (ﷺ) and asked, "O Messenger of Allah! Does anything remain of my responsibility to keep piety to my two parents after their death?" He said, "Yes, four aspects of filial piety remain: praying for them, keeping the promises they made, honoring their friends, and keeping relations with those whom you know only because of them."

3.2. INTERMEDIARIES TO ALLAH

Believers may address Allah with or without an intermediary, although, in truth, there are always several involved. These include: one's personal state, level of obedience, strength of belief, acts committed, sincerity, etc. It is incorrect to imagine that a person who addresses Allah through an intermediary has incorporated another into his worship of Allah. The Prophet (ﷺ) explained this to the Companions once and for all when he said to Abu Bakr al-Siddiq, "Help is not sought with me (i.e. in reality), help is sought with Allah."[46] He did not say to Abu Bakr, "Asking me is forbidden and constitutes association with Allah." What the Prophet (ﷺ) said meant that he is not the source of help, but only the most effective intercessor in obtaining help from Allah.

The meaning of the hadith is elucidated by the Quranic verses, *"You did not throw when you threw, but Allah threw"* (8:17) and, *"Those who swear allegiance unto thee swear allegiance only unto Allah"* (48:10). Furthermore, the Prophet (ﷺ) said, "I did not bear you but Allah bore you." [47]

46 Suyuti, *Jami al-ahadith* 496 #2694. Haythami in *Majma al-zawaid*: "Tabarani related it and its men are those of sound hadith except Ibn Luhay's who is fair (*hasan*).
47 Bukhari and Muslim.

Thus the meaning of the hadith "Help is not sought with me" is:

> (Even if I am the one ostensibly being asked
> for help,) I am not the one being asked for help,
> in reality Allah Himself is being asked.

The hadith "Help is not sought with me" must therefore be interpreted in light of the fact that asking for help applies to whoever the help comes from, especially in respect to the principles of causation and acquisition (or secondary causes). This is what the Arabic means and the Sharia permits. This definition is supported by the hadith in Bukhari (*Kitab al-tawhid*) that discusses intercession on the Day of Resurrection, in which people sought help from Adam (ﷺ), then Moses (ﷺ), then Muhammad (ﷺ) and the last replies, "I can do it."

It is essential to understand that it is not the Prophet (ﷺ) who is the ultimate object of supplication, nor is he the one who grants it; instead he is the best means of forwarding a plea to Allah and having it granted by Allah. This is clear in the Prophet's prayer to Allah, "through Your Prophet (ﷺ) and the prophets before me" and "through those who ask" in the following two hadith:

> On the authority of Abu Said al-Khudri, may Allah be pleased with him: He relates that the Messenger of Allah said, "The one who leaves his house for prayer and then says, O Allah, I ask you by the right of those who ask you and I beseech you by the right of those who walk this path unto you that my going forth bespeak not of levity, pride nor vainglory nor of being done for the sake of repute. I have gone forth in warding off your anger and for seeking your pleasure. I ask you, therefore, to grant me refuge from Hellfire and to forgive me my sins, for no one forgives sins but yourself. Allah will accept for his sake

and seventy thousand angels will seek his forgiveness."[48]

The Prophet (ﷺ) also said, on the authority of
Anas ibn Malik, "O Allah, grant forgiveness to my
mother, Fatima Bint Asad, and make vast for her the
place of her going in [i.e. her grave] by the right of thy
Prophet (ﷺ) and that of those prophets who came
before me."[49]

Tabarani relates this second hadith in *al-Kabir* and *al-
Awsat*. Ibn Hibban and al-Hakim declare it sound. Ibn Abi
Shayba on the authority of Jabir relates a similar narrative.
Similar also is what Ibn Abd al-Barr says on the authority of
Ibn Abbas and Abu Nuaym in his *Hilya*.[50] Haythami says in
Majma al-zawaid, "Tabarani's chain contains Rawh ibn Salah
who has some weakness but Ibn Hibban and al-Hakim declared
him trustworthy. The rest of its sub-narrators are the men of
sound hadith." Imam al-Kawthari says about this hadith in his
Maqalat (p. 410), "It provides textual evidence whereby there is
no difference between the living and the dead in the context of
tawassul, and this is explicit *tawassul* through the prophets,
while the hadith of Abu Said al-Khudri, O Allah, I ask You by
the right of those who ask You, constitutes *tawassul* through
the generality of Muslims, both the living and the dead."

The Prophet (ﷺ) used to say after the two *rakat*s of the
dawn prayer, "O Allah, Lord of Gabriel, of Israfil, of Michael,
and Lord of Muhammad the Prophet (ﷺ), I seek refuge in You
from the fire . . ."[51]

Shaykh Muhammad ibn Alawi al-Maliki said, "The specific
mention of the above in his *dua* is understood as *tawassul*, as if

---

48 This hadith is also related in *Musnad Ahmad* 3:21, Ibn Majah (*Masajid*), al-
Mundhiri in *al-Targhib* 1:179, Ibn Khuzayma in his *Sahih*, Ibn al-Sani, and Abu
Nuaym. Ghazali mentions it in the *Ihya* and Iraqi said: "It is *hasan*." Nawawi mentions
only Ibn al-Sani's two chains in the *Adhkar* and says they are weak (*daif*). However,
Ibn Hajar al-Asqalani says it is *hasan* in *al-Amali al-masriyya* (#54) and also in the
Takhrij of Nawawi's book, explaining that the latter neglected Abu Said al-Khudri's
narration and omitted to mention Ibn Majah's. See Imam Kawthari's remarks on this
hadith below.

49 The Fatima referred to here is the mother of Ali ibn Abi Talib who raised the
Prophet.

50 Related on the authority of Anas Ibn Malik as *al-hafiz* al-Suyuti mentioned in the
Jami al-kabir.

51 Nawawi mentions that this was narrated by Ibn al-Sani and Ibn Hajar graded it fair
(*hasan*) as mentioned by Ibn Allan in his Commentary on the *Adhkar*, Vol. 2 p. 139.

he were saying, "O Allah, I ask You and I seek as means to You Gabriel, Israfil, Michael, and Muhammad the Prophet (ﷺ). Ibn Allan referred to this in his commentary."[52]

3.3. IMAM SHAWKANI

3.3.1. *FATWA* OF IMAM SHAWKANI ON SEEKING MEANS OF APPROACH TO ALLAH (*TAWASSUL*)

Imam Shawkani said in his treatise entitled al-*Durr al-nadid fi ikhlas kalimat al-tawhid*:

> There is no harm in *tawassul* through any one of the prophets or saints or scholars of knowledge . . . One who comes to the grave as a visitor (*zairan*) and invokes Allah alone, using as his means the dead person in the grave, is as one who says, "O Allah, I am asking that you cure me from such-and-such, and I use as a means to You whatever this righteous servant of Yours possesses for worshipping You and striving for Your sake and learning and teaching purely and sincerely for You." Such as this, there is no hesitation in declaring that it is permitted . . . [53]

3.3.2. IMAM SHAWKANI'S DENUNCIATION OF WAHHABIS

Shawkani also says:

> Regarding what those who forbid *tawassul* to Allah through the prophets and the saints cite to support their position, such as Allah's sayings:

> *We only worship them in order that they may bring us nearer* (39:3).

> *Do not call on any other god with Allah, or you will be among those who will be punished* (26:213).

> *Say: Call on those besides Him whom ye fancy; they have no power to remove your trouble from you or to change them. Those unto whom they cry seek for themselves the means of approach to their Lord, which of them shall be the nearest; they hope for His mercy*

---

52 Ibn Alawi al-Maliki, *Mafahim yajib an tusahhah* (Dubai: Hashr Delmuck, 1985) p. 69.
53 Shawkani, *al-Durr al-nadid fi ikhlas kalimat al-tawhid*.

*and fear His wrath: for the wrath of thy Lord is some-
thing to take heed of* (17:57).[54]

These verses are ineffective in supporting their opposition.
Rather, they support exactly the reverse of what they claim,
since the verses are related to another issue. To wit, the verse
"We only worship them in order that they may bring us nearer"
explicitly states that they worship them for that purpose. The
one who makes *tawassul* through a scholar, for example, never
worships him, but knows that he has a special distinction
(*maziyya*) before Allah for being a carrier of knowledge; and
that is why he uses him as a means.

Similarly irrelevant to the issue at hand is Allah's saying,
"Do not call on any other god with Allah." This verse forbids
that one should call upon another together with Allah, as if saying, "O Allah and O so-and-so." However, the one who makes
tawassul through a scholar, for example, never calls on anyone
other than Allah. He only seeks a means to Allah through the
excellent works of one of His servants. In the same way three
men in the cave were blocked by a rock and used their good
works as a means to have their petition answered.

> Narrated by Ibn Umar: Allah's Messenger said,
> "While three persons were traveling, they were over-
> taken by rain and they took shelter in a cave in a
> mountain. A big rock fell from the mountain over the
> mouth of the cave and blocked it. They said to each
> other, 'Think of such righteous deeds which you did
> for Allah's sake only, and invoke Allah by mentioning
> those deeds so that Allah may relieve you from your
> difficulty.' One of them said, 'O Allah! I had my par-
> ents who were very old and I had small children for
> whose sake I used to work as a shepherd. When I
> returned to them at night and milked the sheep, I
> used to start giving the milk to my parents first before
> giving to my children. And one day I went far away in
> search of a grazing place for my sheep, and didn't
> return home till late at night and found that my par-
> ents had slept. I milked my livestock as usual and
> brought the milk vessel and stood at their heads, and
> I disliked to wake them up from their sleep, and I also

disliked to give the milk to my children before my
parents though my children were crying from hunger
at my feet. So this state of mine and theirs continued
till the day dawned. O Allah! If you considered that I
had done that only for seeking Your pleasure, then
please let there be an opening through which we can
see the sky.' So Allah made for them an opening
through which they could see the sky. Then the second person said, 'O Allah! I had a female cousin whom
I loved as much as a passionate man loves a woman.
I tried to seduce her but she refused till I paid her
one-hundred dinars. So I worked hard till I collected
one hundred dinars and went to her with that. But
when I sat in between her legs (to have sexual inter-
course with her), she said, "O Allah's slave! Be afraid
of Allah! Do not deflower me except legally (by mar-
riage contract)." So I left her alone. O Allah! If you
considered that I had done that only for seeking Your
pleasure then please let the rock move a little to have
a wider opening.' So Allah shifted that rock to make
the opening wider for them. And the last person said,
'O Allah! I employed a laborer for wages equal to a
faraq (a certain measure) of rice, and when he had
finished his job he demanded his wages, but when I
presented his due to him, he gave it up and refused to
take it. Then I kept on sowing that rice for him (several times) until I managed to buy, with the price of
the yield, some cows and their shepherd. Later on the
laborer came to me and said, "Be afraid of Allah, and
do not be unjust to me an give me my due." I said to
him, "Go and take those cows and their shepherd." So
he took them and went away. If You considered that I
had done that for seeking Your pleasure, then please
remove the remaining part of the rock.' And so Allah
delivered them."[55]

Also impertinent to the issue is Allah's saying, "Those unto
whom they cry . . ." for it refers to people who call upon those
who cannot fulfill their request, and not upon Allah, Who can.
One who makes *tawassul* through a scholar, for example, never
called except upon Allah, and none other besides Him.
The above shows the reader that objectors to *tawassul* have

55 *Sahih Bukhari,* English translation Vol. 8, Book 73, Number 5.

introduced ineffective evidence in supporting their position. Even more ineffective is their citing the verse:

> The Day when no soul shall have power to do any-
> thing for another: for the Command, that Day, will be
> all with Allah (82:19).

This noble verse states nothing more than the fact that Allah alone decides everything on the Day of Judgment, and that no other will have any say at that time. The maker of *tawassul*, through one of the prophets or one of the scholars, never believes that the one through whom he makes *tawassul* is in partnership with Allah on the Day of Judgment! Whoever believes such a thing of a prophet or non-prophet is in manifest error.

Equally unsupported is their objection to *tawassul* by citing the verses:

> *Not for you is the decision in the least* (3:128),

> *Say: I have no power over good or harm to myself except as Allah wills* (7:188).

These two verses are clear in showing that the Prophet (ﷺ) has no say in Allah's decision and that he has no power to benefit or harm himself in the least, let alone someone else. There is nothing in these two verses that prohibits *tawassul* through him or any other of the prophets, saints, or scholars.

Allah has given His Prophet (ﷺ) the Exalted Station (*al-maqam al-mahmud*)–the station of the Great Intercession (*al-shafaa al-uzma*)—and He has instructed creation to ask for that station for him and to request his intercession. He said to him, "Ask and you shall be granted what you asked! Intercede and you shall be granted what you interceded for!" In His Book He has made clear the fact that there is no intercession except by His leave, and that none shall pretend it except those who please him. Finally, also unsupported is their listing as proof against *tawassul*:

And admonish your nearest kinsmen (26:214).
The Prophet (ﷺ) said, in response to this, "O So-and-so, son of So-and-so, I do not have any guarantee on your behalf from Allah; and O So-and-so, daughter of So-and-so, I do not have any guarantee on your behalf from Allah." For in the preceding there is nothing other than the plain declaration that he cannot benefit anyone for whom Allah has decreed harm, nor harm anyone for whom Allah has decreed benefit, and that he does not have any guarantee from Allah from any of his close relatives, let alone others. This is known to every Muslim. There is nothing in it, however, that prohibits making *tawassul* to Allah through the Prophet (ﷺ), for *tawassul* is a request to the One Who holds power to grant and deny all requests. The petitioner who makes *tawassul* only desires to place, at the front of his petition, what may be a cause for the granting of his petition by the One Who alone gives and withholds, the Owner of the Day of Judgment.

3.4. *FATWA* OF SHAYKH SALIH AL-NAMAN'S ON SEEKING MEANS OF APPROACH TO ALLAH

The following legal opinion on *tawassul* was given by Shaykh Salih al-Naman, the Secretary of the Section of *Ifta* and Religious Education at the Ministry of Religious Endowments (*wizarat al-awqaf*) of the Syrian Arab Republic in the city of Hama on March 22, 1980. It is reproduced in full in the 1992 *Waqf Ikhlas* reprint of Sayyid Ahmad Zayni Dahlan's section of his history of Islam *al-Futuhat al-islamiyya* on the Wahhabi sect entitled *Fitnat al-wahhabiyya*.

Text of the *fatwa*:
Praise belongs to Allah the Lord of the Worlds. Blessings and Peace on our Master Muhammad and on his Family and all his Companions.
From the slave who is poor and in need of Him, the Secretary of Legal Opinions in the city of Hama

(Sham) and the Preacher in the Madfan Mosque, to the brother who asked a question, Sayyid Ashiq al-Rahman in Wilayatullah Abad in India: Warm greetings and blessings. To proceed: You have asked a question on a legal issue, and this answer is given after some delay because I was away in the Hijaz.

You asked about *al-tawassul ilallah taala bi al-anbiya wa al-mursalin* (seeking/using means to Allah the Exalted with/through/by means of the prophets and the messengers) and about *hukmu man tawassal* (the law's position with regard to the person who makes *tawassul*). This is the answer:

Praise belongs to Allah the Exalted! Seeking or using means (*al-tawassul*) to Allah through his Prophet (ﷺ) or the prophets or the Righteous (*al-salihin*) or with the deeds (*amal*) that are done purely for His glorious countenance: There is no legal prohibition against it, because Allah the Exalted said, "*Seek ye the means to Him*" (5:35) and "*Had they but come to thee when they had wronged themselves, and asked Allah forgiveness, and the Messenger had asked forgiveness for them, they would have found Allah Oft-Returning, Merciful*" (4:64), and because the Companions– may Allah be well pleased with them – used to seek a means through Allah's Messenger, as narrated concerning the blind man who used Allah's Messenger as a means (to obtain his request) and his eyes were opened.

The Community has reached consensus on the fact that *tawassul* is permissible as long as one's belief is sound (*idha sahhat al-aqida*), and the consensus of the Community constitutes a legal proof (*ijma al-umma hujjatun shariyya*); as the Prophet (ﷺ) said, "My Community shall not agree on an error." As for the claim of some extremists (*ghulat*) of the Wahhabiyya whereby the law's position with regard to the person who seeks *tawassul* is that it is *shirk* (worshipping other than Allah together with Him), there is no proof for such a claim either legally or rationally, because the person who seeks *tawassul* does not contravene the Prophet's order, "If you ask, ask Allah, and if you seek help, seek help from Allah." Rather, he is asking Him through one beloved to Him in order that his supplication be answered, and this is what our Glorious and Majestic Lord likes from us. How then can we judge that he is committing *shirk* when he is not a *mushrik* (one who commits *shirk*). Such an act the law considers abominable and our religion declares itself innocent of it, since it has been said, "Whoever declares a believer to be an disbeliever has committed disbelief."

Our master Usama ibn Zayd killed a *mushrik* after the latter had said, "There is no god but Allah" (*la ilaha illallah*). When news of this reached Allah's Messenger he condemned our master Usama in the strongest terms and he said to him, "How can you kill him after he said *la ilaha illallah?*" He replied, "But he said it with the sword hanging over his head?" The Prophet (ﷺ) said again, "How can you kill him after he said *la ilaha illallah?*" He replied, "O Messenger of Allah, he said it in dissimulation (*taqiyyatan*)?" The Prophet (ﷺ) said, "Did you split his heart open (to see)?" and he did not cease to reprove him until Usama wished that he had not entered Islam until after he had killed that man so that he might have been forgiven all his past sins through belief.

From this and other narrations we conclude that some of the Wahhabis today may be guilty of hastening to accuse others of disbelief (*takfir*), as they have done in the past with hundreds of thousands in the Hijaz whom they massacred even as they were saying *la ilaha illallah*, and as the Kharijis have done in the time of our Master Ali – may Allah ennoble his countenance.

In short, *tawassul* is not prohibited, rather it is legally commendable (*mustahsanu sharan*), and it is not permitted to cast the label of *shirk* on the believer. This is what will be found in the established books of Islamic law. And Allah knows best."

6 Jumada I 1400
22 March 1980
Signature of the Secretary of *Fatwa*s in Hama
Seal of the Ministry of Religious Endowments
District of the Muhafazat of Hama, Syria

3.5. *FATWA* OF SHAYKH SUHAYL AL-ZABIB'S ON SEEKING MEANS OF APPROACH TO ALLAH

The following *fatwa* on *tawassul* was given by Shaykh Abu Sulayman Suhayl al-Zabibi the Imam of the Mosque of Najjarin in Damascus. It is reproduced in full in the 1992 *Waqf Ikhlas* reprint of Sayyid Ahmad Zayni Dahlan's section of his history of Islam already cited.

Text of the *fatwa*:

> In the Name of Allah the Merciful the Beneficent, and Blessings and Peace upon our Master Muhammad and upon his Excellent and Pure Family and all those who follow them with excellence until the Day of Judgment.
>
> To proceed, you have sent us a letter in which you ask the *fatwa* concerning belief in *tawassul* through the prophets and messengers, Blessings and salutations be upon them, and the text of your question is, Is the person who believes in this (*tawassul*) a *mushrik* (one who worships other than Allah together with Him) or a *kafir* (disbeliever), and is his worship —such as *salat, zakat, hajj*, and *sawm*—sound or void (*sahiha am fasida*)? And you have asked for an exposition from the Glorious Book because it is the first source of legislation, and from the true *sunna* because it holds the second rank in the derivation of proofs after the Noble Quran, and from the Consensus (*ijma*) and the sayings of the pious early generations, may Allah be well pleased with them, because they are closer than us to the full understanding of Allah's Book and the *sunna* of His Messenger.
>
> This is the answer which I give while asking Allah's help and His power and might:
>
> • Belief (*itiqad*) in *tawassul* through the prophets and messengers, blessings and peace be upon them, and through the Righteous Friends of Allah (*al-awliya al-salihin*) upon whose goodness, righteousness, uprightness, and friendship with Allah there is general agreement, is true belief, not disbelief, and I consider it permissible, not forbidden.

• And, the person seeking such as the above as a means to Allah in order that his need be fulfilled is a believer and one who declares the oneness of Allah, not one who worships other than Allah together with Him, and all his acts of worship are sound.

Among the proofs for this from Quran, Allah the Blessed and the Exalted said, *"O ye who believe, fear Allah and seek ye the means to Him"* (5:35) in *Surah al-Maida* verse 35 *juz* 6. Some of the scholars of Islam have derived from this verse a proof for the legality of seeking help and a means to Allah through the righteous ones among His servants, and of considering them a means between Allah the Almighty and His servants for the fulfillment of needs provided that the person making *tawassul* believes that the effective doer (*al-faal*) is Allah and none other. If one thinks otherwise, he has committed disbelief, may Allah the Exalted protect us!

Also among the proofs from Quran for *tawassul* is the saying of Allah the Blessed and the Exalted, *"Had they but come to thee when they had wronged themselves, and asked Allah forgiveness, and the Messenger had asked forgiveness for them, they would have found Allah Oft-Returning, Merciful"* from *Surah al-Nisa* verse 64 *juz* 5. Ibn Kathir said in explanation of this verse, Allah the Exalted advises those who disobey and those who sin, when they commit their mistakes and disobedience, to come to Allah's Messenger and seek Allah's forgiveness in his presence and ask him (the Prophet (ﷺ)) to forgive them. If they do this, Allah relents towards them, grants them mercy, and forgives them," whence He said, *"They would have found Allah Oft-Returning, Merciful."*

Ibn Kathir continues: A large number of the scholars, among whom is Shaykh Abu Mansur al-Sabbagh in his book *al-Shamil*, have mentioned the well-known account related by al-Utbi who said, As I was sitting by the grave of the Prophet (ﷺ), a Bedouin Arab came and said, peace be upon you, O Messenger of Allah! I heard that Allah said, *'If they had only, when they were unjust to themselves, come unto thee and asked Allah's forgiveness, and the Messenger had asked forgiveness for them, they would have found Allah indeed Oft-Returning, Most Merciful,'* so I have come to you asking forgiveness for my sin, seeking your intercession with my Lord (*mustashfian bika ila rabbi*). Then he began to recite poetry:

> O best of those whose bones are buried in the deep
>   earth,
> And from whose fragrance the depth and the
>   height
> have become sweet,
> May my life be the ransom for a grave which thou
>   inhabit,
> And in which are found purity, bounty, and
>   munificence!

Then he left, and I dozed and saw the Prophet (ﷺ) in my sleep. He said to me, O Utbi, run after the Bedouin and give him glad tidings that Allah has forgiven him. This is the end of Ibn Kathir's discourse.

Here now is the proof from the noble hadith. The following hadith was extracted by the following masters of hadith among the Imams: Ibn Khuzayma in his *Sahih* (the rank of which approximates that of *Sahih Muslim*), al-Nasai in his book *Amal al-yawm wa al-layla*, al-Tirmidhi in his *Jami* and he said of it *hasan sahih gharib*, that is, with respect to the fact that only Abu Jafar Umayr ibn Yazid al-Khutami al-Madani al-Basri narrates it, and he is *thiqa* (trustworthy) according to Nasai and Ibn Main, therefore the fact that it is *gharib* does not jeopardize its rank of *sahih*. Ibn Majah also narrated it and confirmed Abu Ishaq [Ibn Rahawayh] who declared it *sahih*, and so did al-Hakim in his *Mustadrak* who said, "It is sound according to the criterion of Bukhari and Muslim," and Dhahabi confirmed him.

From Uthman ibn Hunayf: He was with the Prophet (ﷺ) at the time a blind man came to him complaining of his lack of eyesight, etc. This is a sound hadith in which the Prophet (ﷺ) explicitly orders those who have a certain need to make *tawassul* and call him in his absence—both in his life and after his death. This is precisely what the Companions understood from him, as his order to any given person in the Community is directed to all the Community in every

time as long as there is no proof that it is specific to
an individual. What then if there is proof to the contrary – i.e. that it is not specific to an individual?
Tabarani related in his *Mujam al-kabir* and *Mujam
al-saghir* that a man in need used to try to visit
Uthman ibn Affan frequently, etc. Tabarani said the
hadith was sound and Bayhaqi narrated it in *Dalail
al-nubuwwa* with a good chain."

Abu Sulayman Suhayl al-Zabibi
Imam of Masjid al-Najjarin
(Damascus, Syria)

3.6. FATWA OF MUSTAFA IBN AHMAD IBN AL-HASAN AL-SHATTI AL-HANBALI AL-ATHARI AL-DIMASHQI (1856-1929 CE) ON SEEKING MEANS OF APPROACH TO ALLAH

The following is from the 1994 *Waqf Ikhlas* offset reprint of
al-Shatti's *al-Nuqul al-shariyya fi al-radd ala al-wahhabiyya*
(The legal proof-texts concerning the reply to the Wahhabi
sect).

Allah said:
1. *Fa istaghathahu al-ladhi min shiatihi* (28:15)
"*The man of his [Moses'] own people appealed to him*
[Pickthall: asked him for help] *against his foe.*"[56]
2. *Wa law annahum idh zalamu anfusahum
jauka fa istaghfarullah* . . . (4:64) "If they had only,
when they were *unjust to themselves, come unto thee
[Muhammad] and asked Allah's forgiveness, and the
Messenger had asked forgiveness for them [P: and
asked forgiveness of the Messenger], they would have
found Allah indeed Oft-Returning, Most Merciful.*"
    If a Wahhabi says, "This is specific to him (the
Prophet (ﷺ)) being alive," we say there is unanimity
and the clearest evidences about the Prophet (ﷺ)
being alive in his honored grave.[57]

---

56 The Quranic translation used for this section is that of Yusuf Ali (Revised King
Fahd edition) unless marked by a "P" which indicates that of Muhammad Marmaduke
Pickthall.
    57 In addition to the hadith we have already mentioned, this evidence can be
found in Jalaluddin al-Suyuti's *Anba al-adhkia fi hayat al-anbiya* (The reports of the
enlightened ones concerning the lives of prophets) in *al-Rasail al-ashr* (The ten treatises). Beirut: Dar al-kutub al-ilmiyya, 1409/1989 p. 197-211, also included in his *Hawi*

The rule of this noble verse is applicable now and anytime Allah wills. This is why you see that all scholars recommend reading this verse when visiting his honored grave.[58] This fact cannot be hidden from anybody who has studied the sayings of the scholars in this respect. There is no need to detail it again. Anyone who claims a contrary interpretation has to bring evidence to that effect. And how will he get such evidence when many other verses teach the believers to seek shelter with the Prophet (ﷺ)?

Among such verses are: *al-nabiyyu awla bil muminina min anfusihim* (33:6) *"The Prophet is closer to the believers than their own selves, and his wives are (as) their mothers,"* and *wa ma arsalnaka illa rahmatan lil alamin* (21:107) *"We did not send you except as a Mercy to the worlds."* This is exactly what was understood by the father of humanity, Adam, from the juxtaposition of the name of the Prophet (ﷺ) to Almighty Allah's name. Adam understood that the Prophet (ﷺ) is the intermediary and the means to Him, so he sought intercession through him to his Lord in order to be forgiven; and he was forgiven as has been established.[59]

As for the verses and hadith which have been put forward by the Wahhabis such as the following: *uduni astajib lakum* (40:60) *"Call on [P: pray unto] me; I will answer [P: hear] your prayer"*; *fa firru ila Allah* (51:50) *"Therefore flee unto Allah"*; *wa in yamsask Allahu bi durrin fa la kashifa lahu illa hu* (6:17, 10:107) *"If Allah touch thee with affliction, none can remove it [P: relieve therefrom] but He"*, *"If Allah do touch thee with hurt, there is none can remove it but He"*; *wa nahnu aqrabu ilayhi min habl al-warid* (50:16) *"For We are nearer to him than his jugular vein"*; Hadith: *idha istaanta fa istain billah* "If you

---

li al-fatawi; and Abu Bakr Ahmad ibn al-Husayn al-Bayhaqi, *Kitab ma warada fi hayat al-anbiyai bada wafatihim* (What has been said concerning the lives of prophets after their demise). Beirut: Muassassat Nader, 1410/1990).

58 See for example below, the section on *ziyara*.

59 This is a reference to the hadith of Umar: "When Adam made his mistake. . . " which concerns Adam's seeking forgiveness for the sake of the Prophet Muhammad. This hadith is accepted as authentic by some scholars and rejected as inauthentic by others.

ask for help, then ask help from Allah" etc; these verses do not support the Wahhabis' claim that it is prohibited to use the means of prophets and the pious.
This is very clear. Those who agree among Muslims
about the permissibility and recommendability of
seeking the prophets and pious ones as means never
meant to suppose any effective power as originating
in them. They never believed such a belief at all!
Rather, all Muslims believe that Allah Almighty is the
doer of His own free deliberation, and He alone is the
giver and taker of existence, of benefit, and harm.
This is one of the basic beliefs in Islam. The scholars
never considered seeking the means of prophets and
the pious ones as consisting in *mimman ittakhadha
min dunillahi andadan* or "taking equals other than
Allah" as the Wahhabis have claimed.

Using as evidence to support their school of
thought verses like: *wa la yamurukum an tattakhid-
hu al-malaikata wal-nabiyyina arbaban* (3:80) "[P:]
*And He commanded you not that ye should take the
angels and the prophets for lords*," is a clear manipu-
lation of the meaning of the verse and a use of something out of its proper place. Using the specious argument of those who forbid using an intermediary,
namely that they see the common people often
requesting from the pious ones, whether living or
dead, what should properly be requested only from
Allah Almighty is questionable in our opinion and not
a proven fact as Ibn Taymiyya overtly misrepresents
it in many of his books and treatises. For example, he
discusses something to that effect in relation to the
hadith of the blind man when he begins with the
words: "Concerning this [*tawassul*] there is the
hadith of the blind man . . ." This is a summation of
his opposition to the issue at hand: "And they find
that the common people say to the saint (*wali*): Do
such-and-such for me, and these words that they use
suggest an influence on their part which properly
belongs only to Allah Almighty."

The answer to these challenges is that these con-
fusing expressions must be interpreted figuratively,
and the proof for their having to be taken figuratively is that they originate in the mouth of a pure

monotheist (*muwahhid*). Therefore, if the common person is asked of the soundness of his belief in what he is saying, he will answer that Allah alone is the Most Effective Doer (*al-Faal*) without partner; and that he asks of those great ones who are honored by Allah and brought near Him because they mean by that to use them as their intermediaries to reach their goal which is Allah Almighty. The reason that they have recourse to the pious ones is that the latter have been placed high by Allah Himself and He is the One who holds them in such consideration and they obtain what they desire from Him, as He Himself has said.

We concede that it is good to recommend to the common people that they observe the path of good manners towards Allah Almighty in making their requests; indeed it is a part of ordering the good and forbidding the reprehensible. However, it is not correct for us to forbid them from seeking means and using help in absolute terms. How can that be done when Allah Almighty said, *"The man of his (Moses') own people appealed to him against his foe"* (28:15)?

4. REPUDIATION OF THOSE WHO COMPARE SEEKING MEANS OF APPROACH TO ALLAH AND ASKING FOR INTERCESSION TO THE CHRISTIAN WORSHIP OF JESUS (عليه السلام) AND THE SAINTS, AND OF THOSE WHO LIMIT THE QUANTITY OF PERMISSIBLE INVOCATIONS OF BLESSINGS ON THE PROPHET (صلى الله عليه وسلم)

As for the specious comparison by some "Salafis" of Muslims making *tawassul* through the Prophet (صلى الله عليه وسلم) to the Christian worship of Jesus (عليه السلام), or of Muslims making *tawassul* through saints to the Christian worship of saints, let it be pointed out that Muslims are strict monotheists who worship Allah alone and who can use the blessings of particular acts, times, places, and persons to benefit them, and not as objects of worship. Persistence in making analogies between the doctrines of Muslims and Christians in disregard of their fundamental differences is a characteristic of the enemies of Islam.

One sect in particular among the enemies of *tawassul* are the *bukhala*, or misers, who wish to curtail sending "too much blessings and peace" on the Prophet (ﷺ) on the pretense that it would foster worship of the Prophet (ﷺ). The *bukhala* claim that "praising him too much would be like ascribing a partner to Allah." The Prophet (ﷺ) explicitly declared their status in the hadith when he said, "The miser (*bakhil*) is he before whom my name is mentioned and he does not invoke blessings and peace upon me."[1] Allah said:

> *Verily, Allah and His angels send blessings on the Prophet. O believers! Invoke blessings upon him, and utmost greetings* (33:56).

The *bukhala* have opposed Allah Himself, since Allah Himself is sending His *salat* on the Prophet (ﷺ). If Allah does something, can anyone question Him in that? And if He gives the order to do something, how can one do that thing in excess? Even one *salat* from Allah on His Prophet (ﷺ) is more than all the *salawat jinn* and mankind can ever make, even if they made it forever. For that reason, people can never offer enough *salawat* on the Prophet (ﷺ), nor does our *salat* constitute anything since it is only our asking for more *salat* from Allah on him; *Allahuma salli ala Muhammad*, i.e. "O Allah, we beg You to send Your *salat* on Your Prophet (ﷺ)."

It is a contradiction to suggest that there is too much praise for the Prophet (ﷺ), whose very name is the "Praised One." Scholars have gone so far as to say that Allah has cut the name of the Prophet (ﷺ) from His Own Name, as is explained in the section on the Prophet's Names below. Suffice it to say here that the names of Muhammad, Ahmad, and Mahmud, or "Praised One," "Most Praised," and "Praiseworthy," were never given to any one person before or after him. Allah said, as read by al-Baydawi in his Commentary:[2]

> Allah suffices as witness (that) Muhammad is the Messenger of Allah! (48:28-29).

What differentiates the Muslims from the Jews? The Jews

---

1 Narrated by Tirmidhi (#3546—*hasan sahih gharib*), Nasai, Ibn Hibban, and al-Hakim. Bayhaqi also cites it in *Shuab al-iman* (2:213 #1565-1566).
2 Al-Baydawi, *Anwar al-tanzil* in *Majma al-tafasir* 6:34.

say *la ilaha illallah* but they never like to say *Musa rasulul-lah*. They hold back love for their Prophet Moses (🕮). Christians similarly refuse to say *Isa rasulullah* although for other reasons. Both groups refuse to say *Muhammadun rasul-ullah* and that is where we differ. You cannot be Muslim without acknowledging that Muhammad is the Messenger of Allah, even if you are a believer in Allah. This makes the second part of the *shahada* a requirement for entering Islam, and belief in the Prophet (🕮) a means for salvation from error and punishment. Allah never allows anyone to come to Him saying, "I love You directly." Instead one must obey the order, *"If you indeed love Allah, then follow me, and Allah will love you"* (3:31). Therefore love of Allah can proceed only from love of the Prophet (🕮). Love of the Prophet (🕮) is indicated by praising him and invoking blessings upon him often, as he requested in the hadith *akthiru al-salat alayya* ("Send much blessings upon me") which we cite below.

Scholars have explained that Allah's *salawat* or sending of blessings signifies *rahma*, or mercy, while the believers' salawat or invocation of blessings stands for *dua*, or supplication.[3] The following verse is clear and expresses unrestricted quantity and time in relation to the *salawat* of Allah and His angels. It reads, *"Allah and His angels send blessings, peace, mercy, honor, gifts, and salutations upon the Prophet at all times and with boundless abundance"* (33:56). Allah orders believers to invoke blessings upon him in the same way; that is, incessantly, as far as they are able.

A Muslim does not remember Allah without remembering the Prophet (🕮) also, as the greatest form of remembrance, *la ilaha illallah*, is followed by *muhammadun rasullulah*. This is emphasized by Allah's saying to the people, *"Remember Me and I shall remember you"* (2:152), and elucidated by the hadith, "Whoever invokes blessings upon me once, Allah sends ten blessings upon him."[4] With respect to this connection, *al-hafiz* Sakhawi said:

Just as in the testimony of faith (*shahada*) Allah

---

3 See Ibn al-Arabi's commentary on Tirmidhi's Chapter on the Description of *salat* on the Prophet in *Aridat al-ahwadhi* and Tirmidhi's words to that effect (2:268, 2:271).
4 Narrated by Muslim, Abu Dawud, Tirmidhi (*hasan sahih*), Nasai, Ibn Hibban, Tabarani (*sahih*), and others.

has placed His Messenger's blessed name next to His
own sacred name and has said that he who obeys the
Prophet (ﷺ) obeys Him and he who loves the Prophet
(ﷺ) loves Him, in the same manner He has related
our invoking blessings upon the Prophet (ﷺ) to His
own blessings upon us. Therefore just as Allah said
about His remembrance, "Remember Me and I will
remember you," likewise is His assurance, "Allah
sends ten blessings on the one who invokes a single
blessing on the Holy Prophet (ﷺ)," as it is established
in the sound hadith.[5]

Sakhawi mentions on the same page al-Qadi Abu Bakr ibn
al-Arabi's explanation of the verse, *"Whoso brings a good deed
shall have ten the like of it"* (6:160). He suggests the verse refers
to the good deed of invoking blessings on the Prophet (ﷺ), in
the light of the aforementioned hadith.

Anyone who dares claim that there is any limitation in
quantity, quality, duration, or any other aspect of invoking
blessings and peace on the Prophet (ﷺ) has erred and strayed
from the Quran, the *sunna*, and the religion of Islam. Be
warned, Muslims who love your Prophet (ﷺ)–and all Muslims
love their Prophet (ﷺ)–against those in your midst who dis-
seminate such false advice. Such people are typified by their
inability to differentiate between worship and respect and are
amiss in both. Furthermore, the dissemination of false advice
exemplifies the hatred of non-Muslims for the central symbol of
the religion of Islam, blessings and peace upon him.
Diminishing one's praise of the Prophet (ﷺ) on the pretense
that "it would foster his worship" is to imitate Iblis (Satan),
who refused to prostrate to Adam on the claim that he only worships Allah.

So do those who desire to extinguish Allah's light, but Allah
will perfect His light in spite of them. No one but a non-Muslim
would cringe at the enthusiasm of believers in invoking blessings on their Prophet (ﷺ). Their enthusiasm proceeds directly
from the Prophet's own joy when he received news from Heaven
of the immense mercy granted to his Community for invoking
blessings upon him. Sahl ibn Sad narrates:

5 Al-Sakhawi, *al-Qawl al-badi* p. 132.

Allah's Messenger came out and met Abu Talha. The latter rose and went to him saying, "My father and mother be sacrificed for you, Messenger of Allah! I see joy and delight in your countenance?" The Prophet (ﷺ) said, "Yes, for Gabriel has just come to me saying, 'O Muhammad, whoever among your Community invokes blessings upon you once, Allah records for Him ten meritorious deeds, erases from his register ten evil deeds, and raises him ten degrees because of it.'" al-Sakhawi said, "Our shaykh (Ibn Hajar) graded it *hasan* without doubt."[6]

Another extremely important reason for incessant invocation of blessings on the Prophet (ﷺ) is that it is established in this hadith that "the *dua* or invocation of the believer is suspended between heaven and earth as long as the invocation of blessings and peace upon your Prophet (ﷺ) does not accompany it." Tirmidhi narrates this hadith from Umar, and al-Qadi Abu Bakr ibn al-Arabi comments on it thus:

The chain of men who narrate this is sound and both Malik and Muslim have cited it though not Bukhari. Such an utterance on the part of Umar can only be a prophetic legislation because it is not subject to opinion. It is strengthened by Muslim's narration of the Prophet's words, "If you hear the *muadhdhin*, repeat his words after him then invoke blessings upon me . . . then ask Allah to grant me *al-wasila*."[7]

It is established that invoking blessings on the Prophet (ﷺ) is especially meritorious on Friday according to the following hadith:

Invoke blessings upon me abundantly on Friday because it is a day that is (particularly) witnessed and the angels witness it (abundantly). As soon as a person invokes blessings on me his invocation is shown to me until he ends it." Abu al-Darda said, "Even after (your) death?" The Prophet (ﷺ) replied, "Verily, Allah

---

6 *Ibid.* p. 107.
7 Tirmidhi in the section of his *Sunan* entitled *Sifat al-salat ala al-nabi* and Ibn al-Arabi, *Aridat al-ahwadhi* 2:273-274.

has forbidden the earth to consume the bodies of prophets.[8]

The Prophet (ﷺ) explicitly confirmed that the believer gains by invoking blessings and peace upon him without restriction, even if one ceases all other forms of supplication. This is established in the hadith:

Ubayy ibn Kab said, "After one third of the night the Prophet (ﷺ) used to get up. One such time he said, O People! Remember Allah! The *rajifa* [first blow of the Trumpet] is upon us! The *radifa* [second blow of the Trumpet][9] follows it. Death has come." Ubayy said, *ya rasulallah inni ukthiru al-salata alayka fa kam ajal laka min salati* "O Messenger of Allah, I make much *salawat* upon you as a habit. How much of my prayer should I devote to you?" The Prophet (ﷺ) said, "As much as you like." Ubayy said, "A quarter?" The Prophet (ﷺ) said, "As you like, but if you add to that it will be better for you." Ubayy then mentioned a third, then a half, then two thirds, and always the Prophet (ﷺ) answered, "As you like, but if you add to that it will be better for you." Finally Ubayy said, *ya rasulallah inni uridu an ajala salati kullaha lak* "O Messenger of Allah, I want to devote my entire prayer (i.e. *dua*) to you." Whereupon the Prophet (ﷺ) said, "Then you will be freed from care and your sins will be forgiven." (Another version has, "Then Allah will suffice you in the matter of your worldly life and your hereafter").[10]

---

8 Related by Ibn Majah with a sound chain through Abu al-Darda. Also related with a sound chain from Aws ibn Aws al-Thaqafi by Ahmad, Ibn Abi Shayba, Abu Dawud, al-Nasai, Ibn Majah, al-Darimi, Ibn Khuzayma, Ibn Hibban, al-Hakim (*Sahih,* confirmed by Dhahabi), Tabarani in his *Kabir,* and Bayhaqi in many places, some with the initial addition of the following: "The best of your days is Friday for in it Adam was created and in it his soul was taken back, and in it is the Blowing of the horn, and in it is the Universal Seizure, therefore invoke blessings upon me abundantly on Friday," etc. The first part (concerning the order to invoke more *salat* on Friday and the disclosure of this invocation to the Prophet) is related by Bayhaqi in *Shuab al-iman* through Abi Umama, Anas, and Abu Masud al-Ansari, and by al-Hakim in his *Mustadrak* from the latter. Shafii in his *Musnad* relates the first part only ("Invoke blessings upon me abundantly on Friday") *mursal* from Safwan ibn Salim.

9 These are Mujahid's glosses as related by Bukhari in his *Sahih* (*Riqaq* Ch. 43).

10 Narrated by Tirmidhi (*Qiyama* 23—*hasan sahih*), Ahmad (5:136, 2:527), Abu Dawud (2041), al-Hakim (*sahih*), and al-Bazzar through various chains. Al-Dhahabi narrates it from one of his shaykhs, Tahir ibn Abd Allah al-Ajami, in *Mujam al-shuyukh: al-mujam al-kabir* (Taif: Maktabat al-siddiq, 1408/1988) 1:311 (#342).

The scholars of Islam have offered many commentaries on this important hadith. The following are taken from Shaykh al-Islam Ibn Hajar al-Haytami's *Fatawa hadithiyya* and from the hafiz al-Sakhawi's *al-Qawl al-badi*:

(Haytami:) It is understood from the wording of these narrations that the meaning of the word *salat* in the expression, "I shall devote my *salat* to you" is *dua*–invocation . . . Then the meaning is, "There is a time in which I make *dua* on behalf of myself: how much of that should I devote to you?" If this is established firmly, then consider what the Shaykh al-Islam *al-hafiz* Ibn Hajar said as reported from him by his student *al-hafiz* al-Sakhawi who particularly commended this saying of his, "This hadith constitutes a tremendous principle of the religion for whoever invocakes and supplicates after his recitation and says, 'O Allah, grant our Master Allah's Messenger the reward of this worship.'"[11]

(Sakhawi:) *Salat* in this hadith means invocation (*dua*) and habitual devotion (*wird*) in the following sense: "There is a time in which I supplicate on behalf of myself; how much of that should I devote to you?" The Prophet (☙) did not consider that he should place a limit for him in this respect in order not to close the gate of superabundance for him. Accordingly he persisted in giving Ubayy the choice at the same time as he stressed for him surplus in invocation until Ubayy said, "I shall devote my entire prayer to you." That is, I shall invoke blessings upon you instead of asking anything for myself. Whereupon the Prophet (☙) said, "Then you will be freed from care," that is, do not worry either for your Religion or for your worldly need, because invoking blessings on me includes both remembrance of Allah and rendering honor to the Prophet (☙). The sense of this is an indication to Ubayy that he is actually invoking for himself, as confirmed by the Prophet's report on behalf of his Lord, "Whoever is occupied from beseeching Me because of remembering Me, I shall grant him the best of what I grant those who beseech."[12] Know then that if you

---

11 Al-Haytami, *Fatawa hadithiyya* p. 18.

12 Narrated from Ibn Umar by Tabarani with a "soft" chain *bi sanadin layyin* (i.e. the narrations of one or more of the narrators, although retained, need investigation) according to Ibn Hajar in *Fath al-bari* (Beirut, 1989 ed. 11:161, #6329). Cf. the definition of *layyin* in *Muqaddimat Ibn al-Salah* (p. 239 of the 1974 Egyptian ed.) and

make most of your worship consist in invoking blessings upon your Prophet (ﷺ), Allah will suffice you in
the matter of your worldly life and your hereafter.[13]

However, according to the party of the *bukhala*, the mean
and miserly, to follow the Prophet's advice in this matter
"would foster his worship"! This "Salafi" opinion is far from the
Quran and the *sunna*. In 1,400 years of sending *salawat* on the
Prophet (ﷺ) far more abundantly than is done now, forthright
worship of the Prophet (ﷺ) has yet to occur. How, then, are we
expected to fear its occurrence now? Perhaps the "Salafis" have
forgotten that the Prophet (ﷺ) specifically said, "Those closest
to me in the hereafter are those who invoked blessings upon me
the most (in *dunya*),"[14] and "No people sit at length without
mentioning Allah and invoking blessings on His Prophet (ﷺ)
except they will incur dissatisfaction from Allah (or dissatisfaction on the Day of Rising). If He likes He will punish them and
if He likes He will forgive them?"[15] Instead, they are intent on
inhibiting Muslims from expressing love for their Prophet (ﷺ)
through invoking blessings on him, celebrating his birth, reading his life story, and encouraging each other to know him and
love him more than their own parents and children. These
characteristics are ones that the enemies of this community
wish to eradicate. Also, we know our Prophet (ﷺ), we keep his
status high, we prefer his *sunna* to all other lifestyles, and we
cherish his love among us more dearly than our own lives and
properties.

The following is a list of the principal benefits obtained by

---

Nawawi's *Taqrib* (p. 51 of the 1987 Beirut ed.). However, Ibn Hajar considers this
hadith authentic (11:177, #6345). It is also narrated by Bukhari in his *Tarikh* (2:115),
Abu Nuaym in *al-Targhib* (1337), Ibn Abd al-Barr in *al-Tamhid* (6:46), and Bayhaqi in
Shuab al-iman (1:413-414 #573-574). Also narrated from Abu Said by Tirmidhi (last
hadith of *Thawab al-Quran* #2926, *hasan gharib*) with the wording, "Whoever is occupied by the Quran and My remembrance. . . "

13 Al-Sakhawi, *al-Qawl al-badi* p. 133.

14. Tirmidhi (*hasan gharib*), Ibn Hibban in his *Sahih*, al-Bukhari in his *Tarikh al-
kabir*, Ibn Bashkuwal, Ibn Abi Asim, Abu Nuaym, al-Sakhawi in *al-Maqasid al-hasana*
(#268) and *al-Qawl al-badi* (p. 125), and Bayhaqi in *Shuab al-iman* (2:212-213 #1563-
1564).

15 Narrated from Abu Hurayra and Abu Said al-Khudri by Ahmad, Tirmidhi
(*hasan sahih*) in the beginning of the Book of *Daawat*, Ibn Hibban in his *Sahih*, Ibn
Majah in his *Sunan*, Ibn al-Sani in *Amal al-yawm wa l-layla* p. 443 and by al-Hakim
in the *Mustadrak* (1:496) who said it is *sahih*.

invoking blessings on the Prophet (ﷺ) as compiled by the *hafiz* al-Sakhawi:[16]

> Among the rewards of one who performs *salat* upon Allah's Messenger are the following:
> The *salat*, or blessing, of Allah, His angels, and His Prophet (ﷺ) on that person
> The expiation of his faults
> The purification of his works
> The exaltation of his rank
> The forgiveness of his sins
> The asking of forgiveness for him by his own *salat*
> The recording of rewards the like of Mount Uhud for him and his repayment in superabundant measure
> The comfort of his world and his hereafter if he devotes his entire salat to invoking blessings upon him
> The obliteration of more faults than that effected by the manumission of a slave
> His deliverance from affliction because of it
> The witnessing of the Prophet himself to it
> The guarantee of the Prophet's intercession for him
> Allah's pleasure, mercy, and safety from His anger
> Admission under the shade of the Throne for him
> Preponderance of his good deeds in the balance
> His admission to drink from the Prophet's pond
> His safety from thirst and deliverance from the fire
> His ability to cross the bridge swiftly
> The sight of his seat in paradise before he dies
> Numerous wives in paradise
> The preponderance of his *salat* over more than twenty military conquests
> Its equivalency to giving alms to the needy
> Its being *zakat* and purification for him
> His wealth will increase because of its blessing
> More than one hundred of his needs will be fulfilled through it

16 Sakhawi in his book devoted to the topic entitled *al-Qawl al-badi fi al-salat ala al-habib al-shafi* (The radiant discourse concerning the invocation of blessings on the beloved intercessor).

It constitutes worship
It is the most beloved of all deeds to Allah
It beautifies meetings
It cancels out poverty and material duress
It lets him expect and find goodness everywhere
It makes him the most deserving of goodness
He benefits from it as well as his children and
theirs, as well as those to whom its reward is
gifted in the register of his good deeds
It brings him near to Allah and to His Prophet
It is a light that helps him against his enemies
It cleans his heart of hypocrisy and rust
It commands the love of people and the sight of
the Prophet in dreams
It forbids slander (*ghiba*) against him

In sum, invoking blessings upon the Prophet (ﷺ) is among the most blessed, most meritorious, most useful of deeds in religion and in the life of the world, and carries desirable rewards even beyond this for those who are clever and eager to acquire the deeds which constitute treasures for them, and harvest the most flourishing and glowing of hopes. Indeed, invoking blessings on the Prophet (ﷺ) includes all these tremendous merits, noble qualities, manifold and all-encompassing benefits which are not found together as the result of any other human action or speech except this: *sallahu alayhi wa sallama tasliman kathiran*—may Allah bless him and greet him abundantly.[17]

4.1. SHAYKH AL-ISLAM AL-HAFIZ TAQI AL-DIN AL-SUBKI'S INVOCATION OF SEEKING MEANS TO APPROACH ALLAH

This is *Shaykh al-Islam al-hafiz* Taqi al-Din al-Subki's invocation of *tawassul* through the Prophet (ﷺ). It is taken from his *Fatawa*, Vol. 1 p. 274, at the beginning of the *fatwa* entitled *"Tanazzul al-sakina ala qanadil al-madina"* (The descent of tranquility and peace on the nightlights of Madina)

Transliteration:

al-hamdu lillahi al-ladhi asadana bi nabiyyihi sallallahu

---

17 Al-Sakhawi, *al-Qawl al-badi* p. 98.

alayhi wa sallama saadatan la tabid
wa ashhadu an la ilaha illallahu wahdahu la sharika lahu
al-wali al-hamid
wa ashhadu anna muhammadan abduhu wa rasuluhu
al-hadi ila kulli amrin rashid
sallallahu alayhi wa ala alihi salatan taliqu bi jalalihi
la tazalu talu wa tazid
wa sallama tasliman kathiran ila yawm al-mazid
wa bad fa inna Allaha yalamu anna kulla khayrin ana fihi
wa manna alayya bihi fa huwa bi sababi al-nabiyyi
sallallahu alayhi wa sallama wa iltijai ilayh
· *wa itimadi fi tawassuli ila Allahi fi kulli umuri alayh*
fa huwa wasilati ila Allahi fi al-dunya wa al-akhira
wa kam lahu alayya min niamin batinatin wa zahira.

Translation:
To Allah belongs all praise, Who has blessed us with His Prophet (ﷺ) with an endless felicity.

I bear witness that there is no deity except Allah alone without partner, the Protecting Friend, the Glorious.

I bear witness that Muhammad is His Servant and Messenger, the guide to every upright matter.

May Allah send blessings and peace upon him in a manner befitting His majesty, with a blessing rising ever higher and increasing.

And a superabundant greeting of peace until the Day of the Increase (Day of Judgment).

To proceed: Verily Allah knows that every goodness in my life which He has bestowed upon me is on account of the Prophet (ﷺ) and that my recourse is to him.

And my reliance is upon him in seeking a means to Allah in every matter of mine.

Verily he is my means to Allah in this world and the next. And the gifts of Allah which I owe to him are too many to count, both the hidden and the visible.[18]

This is the language of mainstream Islam. We embrace this language as faultless and accept it. Those in whose hearts

---

18 End of the *fatwa*.

there is a disease find fault with it. And praise belongs to Allah, the Lord of the worlds. Following is a short description of Subki's stature as an imam in Islam, based on Nuh Keller's biographical notice in the *Reliance of the Traveler*:

> Abu al-Hasan Taqi al-Din al-Subki (683-756 / 1284-1355) is the son and father of illustrious scholars and jurists all of the Shafii school. He was a hadith master (*hafiz*), Koranic exegete, and Islamic judge who was described by Ibn Hajar Haythami as "the *mujtahid* Imam whose imamate, greatness, and having reached the level of *ijtihad* (competence for independent legal reasoning) are agreed upon," by Dhahabi as "the most learned, eloquent, and wise in judgment of all the shaykhs of the age," and by Sakhawi as "one of those who are named Shaykh al-Islam" along with his son Taj al-Din. Suyuti says of him, "He authored more than 150 works, his writings displaying his profound knowledge of hadith and other fields and his magisterial command of the Islamic sciences. He educated the foremost scholars of the time, was a painstaking, accurate, and penetrating researcher, and a brilliant debater in the disciplines. No previous scholar attained to his achievements in Sacred Law, of masterful inferences, subtleties in detail, and carefully worked-out methodological principles." Salah al-Din Safadi said of him, "People say that no one like him has appeared since Ghazali, though in my opinion they do him an injustice thereby, for to my mind he does not resemble anyone less than Sufyan al-Thawri." With his vast erudition, he was at the same time a Godfearing ascetic in his personal life who was devoted to worship and *tasawwuf*, though vigilant and uncompromising in matters of religion and ready to assail any innovation or departure from the tenets of the faith of Sunnis.

4.2. DARUD TAJ: INVOCATION OF BLESSINGS UPON THE PROPHET (ﷺ) KNOWN AS "INVOCATION OF THE CROWN"

The following is a transliteration and translation of a

famous invocation of blessings on the Prophet (ﷺ) entitled
Darud taj or "Invocation of the Crown" which is especially well
known in the Indian subcontinent:

Transliteration

allahumma salli ala sayyidina wa mawlana Muhammad
sahibi al-taji wal-miraji wal-buraqi wal-alam
dafi al-balai wal-wabai wal-qahti wal-maradi wal-alam
ismuhu maktubun marfuun mashfuun manqushun fi al-
*   lawhi wal-qalam sayyidi al-arabi wal-ajam*
jismuhu muqaddasun muattarun mutahharun
*   munawwarun fil-bayti wal-haram*
shams al-duha badr al-duja sadr alula nur al-huda
kahf al-wara misbah al-zulam
jamil al-shyam shafi al-umam sahib al-judi wal-karam
wallahu asimuhu wa jibrilu khadimuhu wal-buraqu
*   markabuhu*
wal-miraju safaruhu wa sidratu al-muntaha maqamuhu
wa qaba qawsayni matlubuhu
wal-matlubu maqsuduhu wal-maqsudu mawjuduhu
sayyid al-mursalin khatim al-nabiyyin
shafi al-mudhnibin anis al-gharibin
rahmatun li al-alamin
rahat al-ashiqin murad al-mushtaqin
shams al-arifin siraj al-salikin misbah al-muqarrabin
muhibb al-fuqara wal-masakin
sayyid al-thaqalayn
nabiyy al-haramayn
imam al-qiblatayn
wasilatina fi al-darayn
sahibi qaba qawsayn
mahbub rabbi al-mashriqayni wal-maghribayn
jadd al-hasani wal-husayn
mawlana wa mawla al-thaqalayn
Abi al-Qasimi MUHAMMAD ibni Abdillah
nurin min nurillah
ya ayyuha al-mushtaquna bi nuri jamalihi

sallu alayhi wa alihi wa sallimu taslima
Allahumma salli ala Muhammadin wa ala ali
Muhammadin wa sallim

Translation

O Allah, send blessings and Peace upon our Master and
Patron Muhammad,
The Owner of the Crown and the Ascent and the Buraq and
the Standard,
The Repeller of Affliction and Disease and Drought and
Illness and Pain.
His name is written on high, served and engraved in the
Tablet and the Pen,
The Leader of All, Arabs and non-Arabs,
Whose body is sanctified, fragrant, and pure,
Illumined in the House and the Haram,
The Sun of Brightness, the Full Moon in Darkness,
The Foremost One in the Highest Fields, the Light of
Guidance,
The Cave of Refuge for Mortals, the Lamp That Dispels the
Night,
The Best-Natured One, The Intercessor of Nations,
The Owner of Munificence and Generosity.
Allah is his Protector, Gabriel is his servant.
The Buraq is his mount, the Ascent is his voyage,
The Lote-Tree of the Furthermost Boundary is his station,
Two Bow-Lengths or Nearer is his desire,
His desire is his goal, and he has found his goal,
The Master of the Messengers, the Seal of the Prophets,
The intercessor of sinners, the friend of the strangers,
The Mercy for the Worlds,
The rest of those who burn with love, the goal of those who
yearn,
The sun of knowers, the lamp of travelers,
The light of Those Brought Near,
The friend of the poor and destitute,
The master of Humans and Jinn,

The Prophet of the Two Sanctuaries,
The Imam of the Two *qibla*s,
Our Means in the Two Abodes,
The Owner of *qaba qawsayn*,
The Beloved of the Lord of the Two Easts and the Two
  Wests,
The grandfather of al-Hasan and al-Husayn,
Our patron and the patron of Humans and Jinn:
Abu al-Qasim MUHAMMAD Son of Abd Allah,
A light from the light of Allah.
O you who yearn for the light of his beauty,
Send blessings and utmost greetings of peace
Upon him and upon his Family.

4.3. ANOTHER INVOCATION OF BLESSINGS UPON THE PROPHET (ﷺ)

Below is another well-known invocation of blessings and peace upon the Prophet (ﷺ). Some of the words in it come from the Ansar who greeted the Prophet (ﷺ) with outpourings of joy and acclamation when he entered Madina during his emigration.[19] About this chapter the Companion al-Bara ibn Azib narrates:

> The first people who came to us (in Madina) were Musab ibn Umayr and Ibn Umm Maktum who were teaching Quran to the people. Then there came Bilal, Sad, and Ammar ibn Yasir. After that Umar ibn al-Khattab came along with twenty other Companions of the Prophet (ﷺ). Later on the Prophet (ﷺ) himself came and I had never seen the people of Madina so joyful as they were on the arrival of Allah's Apostle, for even the slave girls were saying, "Allah's Apostle has arrived!" Before his arrival I had already memorized the *Surah* starting with, *"GLORIFY THE NAME OF YOUR LORD, THE MOST HIGH"* (87:1) together with other *Surah*s of *al-Mufassal*.[20]

---

19 See the relevant section in Ibn Kathir's history *al-Bidaya wa al-nihaya*.
20 English *Sahih Bukhari*, Volume 5, Book 58, Number 262. *Al-Mufassal* is a name for the last part of the Quran beginning with *Surah al-Hujurat* or *Surah Qaf* or *Surah al-Ala*.

The Prophet (ﷺ) said, "I was sent to all people without exception"[21] and "I was sent only as Mercy. I was not sent as a punishment."[22]

Invocation:

ya nabi salam alayka
ya rasul salam alayka
ya habib salam alayka
salawatullah alayka

O Prophet, Peace be upon you.
O Messenger, Peace be upon you.
O Beloved, Peace be upon you.
The Blessings of Allah be upon you.

talaa al-badru alayna
min thaniyyat al-wada
wajaba al-shukru alayna
ma daa lillahi da

The full moon has risen over us
From the mountains of al-Wada.
We shall ever give thanks for it
As long as there will be callers to Allah.

anta shamsun anta badrun
anta nurun fawqa nur
anta iksiru al-wujud
anta misbah al-sudur

You are a sun, you are a full moon,
You are light upon light,
You are the quintessence of existence,
You are the lamp in every breast

ashraqa al-badru alayna
fakhtafat minhu al-budur
mithla husnik ma raayna
qattu ya wajh al-surur

The full moon has risen over us
Eclipsing all other moons.
Such as your beauty we have never seen

---

21 *Buithtu ila al-nasi ammatan kaffatan.* Narrated by Ahmad (3:304), Bayhaqi in the *Sunan* (2:433), Ibn Kathir in his *Tafsir* (2:112, 281, 3:389, 4:397, 6:101, 506, 512), Tabarani in the *Kabir* (12:413), and others. Al-Haythami said in *Majma al-zawaid* (8:259-261): "The narrators in Ahmad's chain are trustworthy."

22 Narrated by Muslim in his *Sahih: innama buithtu rahmatun wa lam ubathu adhaban.*

No, never, O face of delight!
ya habibi ya Muhammad
ya arus al-khafiqayn
ya muayyad ya mumajjad
ya imam al qiblatayn
O My beloved, O Muhammad,
O bridegroom of the East and the West,
The one Allah vindicated and exalted,
O Imam of the Two Directions!
ya nabi salam alayka
ya rasul salam alayka
ya habib salam alayka
salawatullah alayka

Abundant Blessings and Greetings of peace upon the Prophet (ﷺ), his Family, and his Companions.

5. ALBANI'S REWORDING OF THE PROPHET'S SUPPLICATION OF SEEKING MEANS TO APPROACH ALLAH

Following is a concise refutation of a recent dissertation by the "Salafi" shaykh Albani entitled *Tawassul: Its Types and Its Rulings*. The translation of the dissertation is currently distributed among English-speaking Muslims by Albani's supporters in order to replace with "Salafi" ideology the understanding of mainstream Islam regarding *tawassul* (seeking means of approach to Allah).[1] It will be seen, with Allah's permission, that the commentary of Albani is instead a proof against "Salafis" and those who follow new teachings instead of holding fast to the *sawad al-azam*, or majority of scholars. Their assertion that "there is disagreement about *tawassul*" and that "we follow proof not scholars" is false. There is no disagreement about *tawassul* among the mainstream Islamic scholars except the objection of some isolated individuals. For example, Ibn Taymiyya declared travel undertaken to visit the Prophet (ﷺ) an act of disobedience. This is not disagreement, but *shudhudh*, or dissent, as classified by Imam Ahmad in reference to the disagreement of the lone scholar against the consensus. Albani must be placed in the same category of dissenters as evidenced by the following argumeny in his book:

1 Albani, *Tawassul* p. 69.

> Imam Ahmad allowed *tawassul* by means of the
> Messenger alone, and others such as Imaam ash-
> Shawkaanee allowed *tawassul* by means of him and
> other prophets and the pious. [Note that he omits to
> mention Imam Malik and Imam Shafii as permitting
> *tawassul* also.] **However we [i.e. Albani and his
> party], as is the case in all matters where there
> is disagreement, follow whatever is supported
> by the proof whatever that is, without blindly
> sticking to the opinions of men.**[2]

The fact that Albani pretends to see proofs that oppose what
the majority understands is characteristic of the "Salafi"
method. As scholars who debate them well know, the "Salafi"
approach is typified by the lack of recognition of any established principles concerning the treatment of primary sources.
Traditionally, mainstream Islamic scholars may familiarize
themselves with the jurisprudence and the principles of
jurisprudence of other schools, but this is impossible for the
"Salafis" to do. They lack any type of method, and constantly
shift from one position to another depending on the issue at
hand. Albani has achieved particular notoriety for his contam-
ination of the field of hadith scholarship with this systematic
unaccountability and free-lance style.

As will be seen in the section on *salat* below, **Albani has
actually suggested altering the prayer** by changing the
words *as-salamu alayka ayyuha al-nabi* to *as-salamu ala al-
nabi* in the *tashahhud*. However, the Prophet (ﷺ) explicitly
said, as related in Bukhari and Muslim, "Pray as you see me
pray," and, "Whosoever innovates something in this matter of
ours (meaning religion), it is *radd* (rejected)." Yet, Albani tries
to alter the *tawassul* through the Prophet (ﷺ), which was valid
for all people and for all times, and reduce it to a one-time supplication that was valid only for the individual in the Prophet's
time who sought intercession. Again, as the Prophet (ﷺ) said,
"There is no preventing what Allah has given, and there is no
avoidance of what He has decreed."[3]

---

2 Albani, *Tawassul* p. 38.
3 Bukhari, Muslim, Abu Dawud, and Ahmad.
."

5.1. ALBANI'S TAMPERING WITH THE HADITH ITSELF

From his book on *tawassul*:

> It is reported by Ahmad and others with an authentic chain of narration from Uthmaan bin Haneef [sic] "that a blind man came to the Prophet (ﷺ) (SAW) and said, 'supplicate to Allaah that He should cure me.' So he (SAW) said, 'if you wish I will supplicate for you and if you wish I will delay that for that is better (and in a narration: and if you wish have patience and that is better for you).' So he said, 'supplicate to Him.' So he (SAW) ordered him to make *wudoo*, and to make *wudoo* well, and to pray two *rakah*s and to supplicate with this *du'aa*, 'O Allaah I ask you and turn to you by means of your Prophet Muhammad, the Prophet of mercy, O Muhammad I have turned by means of you (i.e. your *du'aa*) [sic] to my Lord in this need of mine, so that it may be fulfilled for me, O Allaah accept him as supplicant on my behalf, and accept my supplication for him (to be accepted for me) [sic].' He said, 'So the man did it and he was cured.'"[4]

1 Albani or his translator err on the narrator's name. This is the Companion Uthman ibn Hunayf, not Haneef, and his full name is Abu Amr Uthman ibn Hunayf ibn Wahb of Aws, may Allah be well pleased with him.[5]

2 The wording of the hadith is, "O Muhammad I have turned **with you** (*bika*) to my Lord." It is not "O Muhammad I have turned by means of your *dua* (*bi duaika*) to my Lord." We shall see that this blatant interpolation of another term in lieu of the explicit wording of the hadith is central to Albani's attempt to reword this hadith of the Prophet (ﷺ).[6]

3 The blind man's final words are not "and accept my supplication for him," nor could they be, since he is not praying for the Prophet (ﷺ) but for himself. He is imploring Allah to help him by means of the Prophet's intercession, not by means of his own.

4 Albani, *Tawassul* p. 68.

5 Ibn Hajar, *al-Isaba* 4:220 #5427.

6 The complete and correct translation of this hadith is transcribed above in the section entitled *Seeking Means Through the Prophet*.

The original Arabic is (in one of two versions in Ahmad), *wa tashaffani fihi*, which must be translated, "and join me to him in supplicating You (i.e. join my supplication to his)," as he is well aware that the likelihood of his being heard increases exponentially if it is linked to the Prophet's audience.

One may excuse the false suggestion, that the man not only prays for the Prophet's intercession for him but also for his own interceding for the Prophet (ﷺ), as stemming from a bad translation. However, the poor translation is just as deliberate as the misrendering of "O Muhammad I have turned by means of your *dua* to my Lord." Albani, as will be seen, tries to introduce the supposed *dua* of the blind man on behalf of the Prophet (ﷺ) as additional evidence to support his idea that the *tawassul* in the hadith is by means of supplication (*dua*) and not by means of the person of the Prophet (ﷺ).

Furthermore, the words of the blind man's final request, "and join me to him in supplicating You," are not in all versions. They are not found in the first of Ahmad's two versions, nor in Tirmidhi's version, nor in Ibn Majah's version, nor in Nasai's version, nor in the version retained by Imam Nawawi in his *Adhkar*.[7] Why then does Albani cite it as the primary text instead of assigning it parenthetical mention, as he does with the phrase "and in a narration: and if you wish have patience and that is better for you?" It is because, as has been said, he wants to make the entire hadith revolve around *tawassul* through the *dua* of the Prophet (ﷺ) as opposed to his person, and he wants to use the blind man's own supposed *tawassul* through his own *dua* as additional evidence of his claim, as we see below.

5.2. ALBANI'S DISSENT AND CONTEMPT FOR THE SCHOLARS

Albani continues:

> The opponents hold that this hadeeth shows that it is permissible to make *tawassul* in *du'aa* by the sta-

---

7 Nawawi, *al-Adhkar* (Taif: Matkata al-muayyad, 1408/1988) p. 239 #562.

tus of the Prophet (SAW) or other pious people, since
the Prophet (SAW) taught the blind man to use him
as a means of nearness in his *du'aa*, and the blind
man did that and his sight was restored.[8]

Observe how Albani says "the opponents," although it is he
who has brought opposition to something established in Islam.
It is he who invented that it is not through the Prophet's sacred
status (*hurma*) or person (*dhaat*) that *tawassul* is permissible,
but through his supplication (*dua*). He is in open contradiction
to the understanding of the Salaf, including Mujahid, Imam
Malik,[9] Imam al-Shafii,[10] Imam Ahmad,[11] Ibrahim al-Harbi,
al-Shawkani (as we have already seen), Ibn al-Jawzi, Nawawi,
Ibn al-Humam, and Ibn al-Qayyim (as seen below).
Albani again:

> As for us, than [*sic*] we hold that the hadeeth has
> no proof for them concerning this form of *tawassul*
> about which there is disagreement, which is seeking
> nearness by means of his person. Rather it is a fur-
> ther proof for the third type of lawful and prescribed
> *tawassul* which we have spoken of previously [i.e.
> through the *du'aa* of another person], since the
> *tawassul* of the blind man was through means of his
> (SAW) *du'aa*, and the proofs for what we say are
> many being contained in the hadeeth itself, most
> importantly:[12]

On the contrary, Muslims believe as Ibn al-Jawzi said, that

---

8 Albani, *Tawassul* p. 69.

9 Imam Malik said to al-Mansur inside the Prophet's Mosque in Madina: "Face
him [the Prophet] and ask for his intercession (*istashfi bihi*)." It is cited by al-Qadi Iyad
in *al-Shifa* (2:92-93) with a sound (*sahih*) chain, and also cited by al-Samhudi in
Khulasat al-Wafa, Subki in *Shifa al-siqam*, Qastallani in *al-Mawahib al-laduniyya*,
Ibn Jamaa in *Hidayat al-salik*, and Haytami in *al-Jawhar al-munazzam* and *Tuhfat al-
zuwwar*. Seel also Ibn Abd al-Hadi in *al-Sarim al-munki* p. 244. Ibn Jamaa says in
Hidayat al-salik (3:1381): "It is related by the two *hafiz* Ibn Bashkuwal and al-Qadi
Iyad in *al-Shifa* after him, and no attention is paid to the words of those who claim that
it is forged purely on the basis of his idle desires."

10 Imam Shafii in his *Diwan* declared his reliance on *tawassul* through the
Prophet's family, and he also made *tawassul* through Imam Abu Hanifa, as related by
al-Haytami respectively in *al-Sawaiq al-muhriqa* in many places and *al-Khayrat al-
hisan* p. 63.

11 As reported by Ala al-Din al-Mardawi in his book *al-Insaf fi marifat al-rajih
min al-khilaf ala madhhab al-Imam al-mubajjal Ahmad ibn Hanbal* (3:456). [See
above].

12 Albani, *Tawassul* p. 69.

it is through the Prophet's person and status and not only through his supplication (*dua*) that one makes *tawassul*. This is clear from the following excerpt:[13]

> Part of the exposition of his superiority to other prophets is the fact that Adam asked his Lord through the sacred status (*hurma*) of Muhammad that He relent towards him, as we have already mentioned.[14]

The importance of this remark does not lie in the veracity of the hadith, which is a separate discussion–although Ibn al-Jawzi clearly considers it authentic, but in Ibn al-Jawzi's stating that *tawassul* is correct as made through the status of the Prophet (ﷺ). This is enough of an indication that Ibn al-Jawzi's *aqida* or doctrine concerning *tawassul* fully contradicts that of Albani and his followers. It comes down to deciding who is closer to following the *sunna*; the Imams, *huffaz* and historians on the one hand, or the polemicist and scholar of books?

Indeed Albani's position is not founded on the explicit words of the hadith, but upon their figurative interpretation. The hadith clearly says, *bi nabiyyika*, i.e. with/by means of/through Your Prophet (ﷺ). Although it is obvious that this does not mean "through the *dua* of your Prophet (ﷺ)," Albani does not provide any justification for his recourse to figurative interpretation in a matter where the literal meaning is clear and true. Albani states:

> The reason the blind man came to the Prophet (SAW) was for him to make supplication (*du'aa*) for him, as he said, 'Supplicate Allaah that He should cure me.' So he sought to use his (SAW) *du'aa* as a means of nearness to Allaah, the Most High, since he knew that his (SAW) supplication was more likely to be accepted by Allaah than the du'aa of others, and if the intention of the blind man was to seek nearness to Allaah by means of the Prophet's (SAW) person or status or his right, then he would have had no need to go to the Prophet (SAW), or to ask him to make *du'aa* for him, rather he would have sat in his house, and sup-

---

13 Ibn al-Jawzi from his chapter concerning the Prophet's superiority over the other prophets in *al-Wafa*. (Beirut: Dar al-kutub al-ilmiyya, 1408/1988).
14 *Ibid.* p. 365.

plicated to his Lord saying, for example, 'O Allaah I
ask You by the status of your Prophet and his station
with You, that You cure me and enable me to see.'
    But that is not what he did. Why? because he was
an Arab and knew very well the meaning of 'tawassul'
in the Arabic language, and knew that it was not a
word said by a person with a need, mentioning the
name of a person as an intermediary, rather it had to
include coming to one whom he believed to be pious
and have knowledge of the Book and the Sunnah and
ask him to make du'aa for him.[15]

This argument is entirely speculative and the Sharia is not
derived from speculation. The facts are clear. The ruling is not
derived only from the fact that the blind man came to the
Prophet (ﷺ) but from the entirety of the hadith. The blind man
came asking for the Prophet's *dua*, and the Prophet (ﷺ) taught
him a form of *dua* that he should make after performing *wudu*
and praying two *rakat*. In the *dua*, the Prophet (ﷺ) further
taught him to make *tawassul* with certain clear and explicit
words. These same words were used by a man in need during
the time of Uthman ibn Affan, after the life of the Prophet (ﷺ).
Was the man in need not also an Arab who knew very well the
meaning of 'tawassul' in the Arabic language?

    Concerning the hadith of the man in need that we have
already cited in full earlier, Shaykh Yusuf al-Rifai wrote in his
rebuttal to a "Salafi" critic, "This is an explicit, unequivocal
text from a prophetic Companion proving the validity of *tawassul* through the dead."[16] Shaykh Muhammad al-Hamid (1910-
1969) has written, "As for calling upon the righteous (when
they are physically absent, as in the words *Ya Muhammad* in
the hadiths of Uthman Ibn Hunayf), *tawassul* to Allah Most
High through them is permissible, the supplication (*dua*) being
to Allah Most Glorious, and there is much evidence for its permissibility. Those who call on them intending *tawassul* cannot
be blamed."[17] Are Shaykh al-Sayyid Yusuf al-Rifai, Shaykh
Muhammad al-Hamid, and Shaykh Abd Allah al-Ghumari not
also Arabs who know very well the meaning of *tawassul*?

---

15 Albani, *Tawassul* p. 69.
    16 Shaykh Yusuf al-Rifai, "The Evidence of the Sunni Community" (*Adilla ahla al-
sunna wa al-jamaa*).
    17 Nuh Keller in his "Rebuttals of Falsehoods" (*Ruduf ala abatil*). Both quoted in
The Reliance of the Traveller p. 935-940.

Were Imam Ahmad, Shawkani, and Ibn al-Jawzi not also Arabs who knew very well the meaning of *tawassul*? What about Imam Nawawi and Ibn al-Humam, who are cited below as having instructed every visitor to the Prophet (ﷺ) in Madina to seek him as a means in *tawassul*? Are they not Arabs who knew very well the meaning of *tawassul* in the Arabic language? All these major scholars did not seem to experience the same problem as Albani with the language of *tawassul*, nor with the fact that *tawassul* is said by a person along with the name of another person as intermediary.

Albani continues:

> The Prophet (SAW) promised that he would make du'aa for him, after advising him of what would be better for him, and this was his (SAW) saying, 'If you wish I will supplicate for you, and if you have patience that is better for you.' And this second matter is what he (SAW) indicated in the hadeeth which he narrated from His Lord, the blessed and Most High, that He said, 'when I afflict My servant in his two beloved ones, that is his eyes, and he has patience, then I give him paradise in place of them.' [Reported by al-Bukhaaree (transl. 7/377/no.557) from Anas, quoted in as-Saheehah (2010)].
>
> The blind man's insistence that he (SAW) should supplicate for him, as he said, 'Supplicate to Him.' Which means that the Messenger (SAW) definitely did make supplicate for him, since he (SAW) was the best at fulfilling a promise and he had already promised to make *du'aa* for him if he wished as has preceded, and he wanted *du'aa* from him, and so the point is established. Also the Prophet (SAW), out of his mercy and desire that Allaah, the Most High, should answer his *du'aa* for him, guided the blind man to using the second type of lawful and prescribed tawassul, which is tawassul by means of righteous actions, in order to combine the different types of good.
>
> So he ordered him to make *wudoo*, and to pray two *rakah*s, and then to make *du'aa* for himself . . . [18]

---

18 Albani, *Tawassul* p. 70.

... In the words taught to him by the Prophet (ﷺ), which specifically consist of asking Allah through the Prophet (ﷺ) himself and his status. That is the essence of the *dua* taught by the Prophet (ﷺ), and of the entire hadith.

Albani again:

> ... and these are acts of obedience to Allaah, the One free of all blemish or defect, and the Most High, which he offered along with the *du'aa* of the Prophet (SAW) on his behalf, and this falls under Allaah, the Most High's Saying, 'Seek means of approach (*waseelah*) to Him' (5:35) as has preceded.
>
> The Messenger (SAW) did not suffice with making *duaa* for the blind man, as he had promised, he also gave him an action to perform which involved obedience to Allaah, the One free of all blemish and defect, the Most High, and drawing near to Him, so that the affair would be complete from all angles, and nearer to acceptance and being pleasing to Allaah, the One free of all blemish and imperfections, and the Most High, therefore the whole event revolved around *du'aa*, as is clear and contains nothing of what they mention.
>
> Shaikh al-Ghumaaree[19] is ignorant of this or pretends to be, since he says in '*al-Misbaah*' [p. 24], "'... If you wish I will make *duaa* for you", means, "if you wish I will teach you a *duaa* which you can make and will repeat it to you," this explanation is binding so that the start of the hadeeth agrees with its end.'
>
> I say that this explanation is futile due to many reasons, from them that the blind man asked him (SAW) to make *duaa* for him, not to teach him a *duaa*, and since his (SAW) saying to him, 'And if you wish I will make *du'aa*' was an answer to his request, it was then definitely a request for *du'aa*, and this has to be, and this is the meaning which agrees with the end of the hadeeth, which is why we find that al-Ghumaaree does not try to explain his saying at the end, 'O Allaah accept him as a supplicant for me, and accept my supplication for him (to be accepted for me),' since this

---

19 Abd Allah ibn Muhammad ibn al-Siddiq al-Ghumari, a *muhaddith* and Sufi shaykh from Morocco and the shaykh of Hasan Ali al-Saqqaf.

clearly shows that his *tawassul* was through the *duaa* of the Prophet (SAW) as we have shown in what has preceded.[20]

Rather, the end does confirm that the essence of this *dua* revolves around the Prophet's intercession, and that is what making *tawassul* through him means. Shaykh al-Ghumari is right when he says that the Prophet (ﷺ) taught the *dua* of *tawassul* as an answer to the blind man's request for *dua*, since the *dua* of *tawassul* is the main lesson of this hadith and the means through which Allah fulfills the Prophet's own *dua* and returned the blind man's sight to him. Nor does the fact that the blind man asked the Prophet (ﷺ) to make *dua* for him preclude the Prophet (ﷺ) from teaching him (and through him all Muslims) that *dua*, as well as addressing his initial request. The Prophet (ﷺ) is by essence the Teacher and Purifier of the Community:

> *Truly Allah was gracious to the believers when He raised up among them a Messenger from themselves, to recite to them His signs and to purify them, and to teach them the Book and the Wisdom, though before they were in manifest error* (3:164).

To insist that the Prophet (ﷺ) could not have been acting in a generally didactic way and was making the *dua* for the blind man only because that is all that the blind man wanted, is to act like the man who said to the Prophet (ﷺ), "Teach me something (about Islam)!" and did not realize that the Prophet's answer, "Do not get angry," constituted a universal Islamic teaching.[21] Yet this is what Albani insists, in order to reduce the hadith to a one-time occurrence that bears no significance to the *umma* at large, and in order to annihilate its availability to all Muslims as a universal and enduring *dua* of *tawassul*.

One great characteristic of Islam is that the overwhelming majority of the Prophet's guidance, teachings, and miracles are valid for all time—the greatest being the Glorious Quran—and not limited to the time of the Companions or to some individu-

---

20 Albani, *Tawassul: Its Types and Rulings* p. 70-71.
21 Related by Bukhari. Cf. Nawawi's *Forty Hadith* #16.

als among them! To believe otherwise is to rob Islam of its primacy as the religion that pleases Allah and to place it on a par with Christianity and Judaism as an abrogated religion, and we seek refuge in Allah from such aberrant suggestions.

> Then he [Ghumari] says, 'Even if we admit that the Prophet (SAW) made *duaa* for the blind man, then that does not prevent those hadeeth from being generalised to include others.
> 'I say that this is clear error, since no one prevents the hadeeth from applying to other then [*sic*] the blind man, from those whom the Prophet (SAW) made *du'aa* for. However since *du'aa* from him (SAW) after he left to join the highest company is something that those seeking *tawassul* for all various needs and desires do not know about, and also they themselves do not seek *tawassul* by his (SAW) *du'aa* after his death, therefore the ruling is different, and this admission of al-Ghumaaree is a proof against him.[22]

Observe the aberration of Albani's declaration that "*du'aa* from him (SAW) after he left to join the highest company is something that those seeking *tawassul* for all various needs and desires do not know about," when it is established in the authentic hadith that the Prophet (ﷺ) continually makes *dua* and asks forgiveness for his *umma* and makes *tahmid* (*al-hamdu lillah*) even in the grave:

> My life is a great good for you, you will relate about me and it will be related to you, and my death is a great good for you, your actions will be presented to me (in my grave) and if I see goodness I will praise Allah, and if see other than that I will ask forgiveness of Him for you.[23]

22 Albani, *Tawassul: Its Types and Rulings* p. 71-72.

23. Haytham says in *Majma al-zawaid* (9:24 #91): "Al-Bazzar relates it and its sub-narrators are all sound (*rijaluhu rijal al-sahih*)." Qadi Iyad cites it in *al-Shifa* (1:56 of the Amman edition). Suyuti said in his *Manahil al-safa fi takhrij ahadith al-shifa* (Beirut 1988/1408) p. 31 (#8): "Ibn Abi Usama cites it in his *Musnad* from the hadith of Bakr ibn Abd Allah al-Muzani, and al-Bazzar from the hadith of Ibn Masud with a sound (*sahih*) chain."Ibn al-Jawzi mentions it through Bakr and then again through Anas ibn Malik in the penultimate chapter of the penultimate section of *al-Wafa*, and also mentions the version through Aws ibn Aws with a sound chain: "The actions of human beings are shown to me every Thursday on the night of (i.e. preceding) Friday. See also *Fath al-bari* 10:415, al-Mundhiri's *al-Targhib wal-tarhib* 3:343, and *Musnad Ahmad* 4:484.

Observe also how Albani boldly claims, "they themselves do not seek *tawassul* by his (SAW) *du'aa* after his death." This is clear and manifest error. As has been shown in many places already, the Companions sought *tawassul, tabarruk, istisqa,* and *istishfa*, both through his person and through his *dua* after his death.

This additional proof against misguidance, is confirmed by Malik al-Dar's narration of the Companion Bilal Ibn al-Harith's request to the Prophet (ﷺ) that he make *istisqa* (prayer and *dua* for rain) on behalf of his Community:

The people suffered from drought during the successorship of Umar, whereupon a man came to the grave of the Prophet (ﷺ) and said, "O Messenger of Allah, ask for rain for your Community, for verily they have but perished . . ."[24]

Let it be noted here that in his obstinacy in asserting that the Companions did not seek *tawassul* by the Prophet's *dua* after his death, Albani went far afield trying to disprove the authenticity of this hadith:

> We do not accept that this story is authentic since the reliability and precision of Maalik al-Daar is not known, and these are the two principle [sic] conditions necessary for the authenticity of any narration, as is affirmed in the science of hadeeth. Ibn Abee Haatim mentions him in *al-Jarh wat-ta'deel* (4/1/213) and does not mention anyone who narrates from him except Aboo Saalih. So this indicates that he is unknown, and this is further emphasized by the fact that Ibn Abee Haatim himself, who is well known for his memorisation and wide knowledge, did not quote anyone who declared him reliable, so he remains unknown. Then this does not contradict the saying of al-Haafidh, " . . . with an authentic chain of narration, from the narration of Aboo Saalih as-Saman . . ." since we say, It is not declaration that all of the chain of narration is authentic (saheeh), rather only that it is so up to Aboo Saalih. If that were not the case then he would not have started mentioning the chain of narration from Aboo Saalih. Rather he would have begun, "From Malik ad-Daar . . . and its chain of narration is

---

24 This hadith in which Ibn Hajar said, "Ibn Abi Shayba related with a sound chain from the narration of Abu Salih al-Saman from Malik al-Dar who was Umar's treasurer," is cited above.

authentic." But he said it in the way that he did to draw attention to the fact that there was something requiring investigation in it. The scholars say this for various reasons. From these reasons is that they may not have been able to find a biography for some narrator(s) and therefore they would not permit themselves to pass a ruling on the whole chain of narration . . .[25]

1 The above is disproved by Ibn Sad's (d. 230) biographical notice on Malik al-Dar:

> Malik al-Dar: Umar ibn al-Khattab's freedman. He narrated from Abu Bakr and Umar. He was known.[26]

2 It is further disproved by the *hafiz* al-Khalili's (d. 445) notice on Malik al-Dar:

> Malik al-Dar: *muttafaq alayh athna alayhi al-tabiun*–He is agreed upon (as trustworthy), the Successors have approved highly of him.[27]

3 It is even further disproved by Ibn Hajar al-Asqalani's biographical notice on Malik al-Dar:
Malik ibn Iyad: Umar's freedman. He is the one named Malik al-Dar. He has seen the Prophet (ﷺ) and has heard narrations from Abu Bakr al-Siddiq. He has narrated from Abu Bakr and Umar, Muadh, and Abu Ubayda. From him narrated Abu Salih al-Saman and his (Malik's) two sons Awn and Abd Allah . . . [28]

Bukhari in his *Tarikh* narrated through Abu Salih Dhakwan from Malik al-Dar that Umar said during the period of drought, "O my Lord, I spare no effort except in what escapes my power!" Ibn Abi Khaythama also narrated it in those words but in a longer hadith:

25 Albani, *Tawassul: Its Types and Rulings* p. 120.
26 Ibn Sad, *Tabaqat* 5:12.
27 Abu Yala al-Khalil ibn Abd Allah al-Khalili al-Qazwini, *Kitab al-irshad fi marifat ulama al-hadith*, ed. Muhammad Said ibn Umar Idris, 1st ed., 3 vols. (Riyad: Maktabat al-rushd, 1989), as quoted in Abd Allah al-Ghumari, *Irgham al-mubtadi al-ghabi bi jawaz al-tawassul be al-nabi,* ed. Hasan Ali al-Saqqaf, 2nd ed. (Amman: Dar al-imam al-Nawawi, 1412/1992) p. 9.
28 Ibn Hajar al-Asqalani, *al-Isaba fi tamyiz al-sahab.*

The people suffered a drought during the time of Umar, whereupon a man came to the grave of the Prophet (鑾) and said, "O Messenger of Allah, ask Allah for rain for your Community." The Prophet (鑾) appeared to him in a dream and told him, "Go, see Umar and tell him, 'you will be watered, and, you must put your nose to the grindstone,' (*alayk al-kaffayn*)!" (The man went and told Umar.) Then Umar wept and exclaimed, "O my Lord, I spare no effort except in what escapes my power!"

We have also narrated in the *Fawaid* of Dawud ibn Amr and *al-Dabbi* compiled by al-Baghawi in the narration of Abd al-Rahman ibn Said ibn Yarbu al-Makhzumi from Malik al-Dar: he said, "Umar ibn al-Khattab summoned me one day. He had with him a purse of gold containing four hundred dinars. He said, 'Take this to Abu Ubayda,'" and he mentioned the rest of the story.

Ibn Sad mentioned him (Malik al-Dar) in the first layer of the Successors among the people of Madina and said, "He narrated from Abu Bakr and Umar, and he was known." Abu Ubayda said of him, "Umar put him in charge of the dependents in his household. When Uthman succeeded him, he put him in charge of financial allotments and he was then named Malik of the House."

Ismail al-Qadi related from Ali ibn al-Madini: "Malik al-Dar was Umar's treasurer."[29]

4 It is also further disproved by Hasan al-Saqqaf's rebuttal of Albani's discourse and method in his treatment of this hadith:[30]

Albani has declared this sound hadith weak upon pretexts frailer than a cobweb in his *tawassul*. He has claimed that Malik al-Dar is unknown (*majhul*) and has reproduced only his biographical notice from Ibn Abi Hatim's *Kitab al-jarh wa al-tadil* in order to give his readers the impression that only one man has narrated from Malik al-Dar, and that is Abu Salih al-Saman. And it has been decided by Albani on the basis

29 Ibn Hajar, *al-Isaba* (Calcutta 1852 ed.) 6:164 #8350.
30 See Saqqaf's preface to Abd Allah al-Ghumari's refutation of Albani entitled *Irgham al-mubtadi al-ghabi bi jawaz al-tawassul bi al-nabi* (The compulsion of the ignorant innovator with the permissibility of seeking means with the Prophet).

of what he reproduces from one of the scholars that a man remains "unknown" until two or more narrate from him. In order to help his cause he mentioned that al-Mundhiri and al-Haythami did not know Malik al-Dar, that he is therefore unknown, and that a chain of transmission containing an unknown is unsound. Then he began to brag saying, "This is a critical piece of information which none will know but those who have practiced this science." As for us we say to him, "Rather this is deliberate concealment (*tadlis*) and deceit and treachery which none commits except one whose heart is filled with spite and enmity against the *sunna* and *tawhid* and its people" . . .

If al-Mundhiri and al-Haythami declared that they did not know him,this means that they could not declare him either trustworthy or unreliable. However, there are those who do know him, such as Ibn Sad, and Bukhari, and Ali ibn al-Madini, and Ibn Hibban, and *al-hafiz* Ibn Hajar al-Asqalani, and others whose argument is retained.

It is a wonder that Albani approves the statement of those who don't know Malik al-Dar's case, selects it, and prefers it to the statements of those who do know it, which he conceals and with which he dislikes that anyone be acquainted.

What is cited below from the sayings of the Imams among the masters of hadith who have recognized Malik al-Dar as reliable is enough to confirm what al-Sayyid Abd Allah al-Ghumari and other hadith scholars as well as some of those who work with hadith have said: namely, that Albani knows the correct facts in many matters but . . . is not to be relied upon for (assessing) a single hadith. This is the explicit position of many of the scholars such as the three muhaddiths al-Sayyid Ahmad al-Ghumari, al-Sayyid Abd Allah al-Ghumari, and al-Sayyid Abd al-Aziz; the shaykh Abd al-Fattah Abu Ghudda; the muhaddith of India and Pakistan Habib al-Rahman al-Azami; Shaykh Ismail al-Ansari; Shaykh Muhammad Awwama; Shaykh Mahmud Said; Shaykh Shuayb Arnaut; and tens of others among the experts in this field and those that deal with it. The People of Hadith therefore witness that that man's word is not relied upon in the authentication and weakening of hadith because he authenticates and weakens according to whim and mood, not scientific rules, and whoever examines his sayings and writings can verify this.

5.3. A REFUTATION OF ALBANI FROM IMAM NAWAWI AND IMAM IBN AL-HUMAM AL-HANAFI

A further proof that *tawassul* through the Prophet (ﷺ) after his time is universally recognized and encouraged in the Sharia is Imam Nawawi's description of the etiquette of visiting the Prophet's grave after the pilgrimage. He says:[31]

> [After giving *salam* to the Prophet, Abu Bakr, and Umar] Then he [the visitor] returns to his initial station opposite the Prophet's face, **and he uses the Prophet as his means with regard to himself** (*fa yatawassalu bihi fi haqqi nafsihi*), **and seeks his intercession before his exalted and mighty Lord** (*wa yatashaffau bihi ila rabbihi subhanahu wa taala*) . . . and he avails himself of this noble spot, and glorifies and praises and magnifies Allah and invokes blessings on His Messenger. Let him do all that abundantly.[32]

Nawawi also says:[33]

> [The visitor stands and greets the Prophet (ﷺ), then he moves to greet Abu Bakr and Umar] Then he returns to his original position, directly in front of Allah's Messenger, and he uses the Prophet (ﷺ) as his means with regard to himself (*fa yatawassalu bihi fi haqqi nafsihi*), and seeks his intercession before his exalted and mighty Lord (*wa yatashaffau bihi ila rabbihi subhanahu wa taala*) and one of the best things that he can say is what has been narrated by our col-

---

31 Nawawi, Book of *Hajj* in the *Adhkar*.

32 Nawawi, *al-Adhkar* (Taif ed.) p. 262.

33 Nawawi, in the part devoted to visiting the Prophet in his book on pilgrimage entitled *al-Idah fi manasik al-hajj*.

leagues on al-Utbi's authority, and they admired what he said:

As I was sitting by the grave of the Prophet (ﷺ), a Bedouin Arab came and said, "Peace be upon you, O Messenger of Allah! I have heard Allah saying, "*If they had only, when they were unjust to themselves, come unto thee and asked Allah's forgiveness, and the Messenger had asked forgiveness for them, they would have found Allah indeed Oft-Returning, Most Merciful*" (4:64), so I have come to you asking forgiveness for my sin, seeking your intercession with my Lord . . ." [34]

Similarly the Hanafi *faqih* Kamal al-Din ibn al-Humam said:[35]

wa yasalu allaha hajatahu mutawassilan ilallah bi hadrati nabiyyihi thumma qala yasalu al-nabiyya sallallahu alayhi wa sallam al-shafaata fa yaqulu ya rasulallah as aluka al-shafaata ya rasulallah atawassalu bika ilallah

Then let him ask Allah for his need, using Allah's Prophet (ﷺ) as his means to Allah; (then he said), Let him ask the Prophet (ﷺ) for his intercession and say, O Messenger of Allah, I am asking you for your intercession; O Messenger of Allah, I am using you as my means to Allah.

Therefore it cannot be more clear that Albani is innovating in:

1 Claiming that *tawassul* is no longer made by asking for the Prophet's supplication (*dua*) after he left this world (*dunya*); and

2 Claiming that seeking means of approach to Allah (*tawassul*) is not made through the Prophet's person or status.

Albani states:

That in the *duaa* which Allaah's Messenger (SAW) taught him to say occurs, 'O Allaah accept him

---

34 Nawawi, *al-Idah fi manasik al-hajj* (Damascus: Dar ibn Khaldun, n.d.) p. 144. See also a similar passage in Nawawi's *Majmu* (8:212f).

35 Kamal al-Din ibn al-Humam, *Fath al-qadir* (2:337), book of *hajj*, chapter on visiting the Prophet.

as a supplicant [intercessor] for me', and it is impossible to take this to mean *tawassul* by his (SAW) person, or his status, or his right, since the meaning is, 'O Allaah accept his (SAW) supplication for You to restore my sight.'[36]

The complete words of the *dua* are as follows:

> O Allah I ask you and turn to you by means of your Prophet Muhammad (ﷺ), the Prophet of Mercy. O Muhammad (ﷺ) I turn by means of you to my Lord in this need of mine, so that it may be fulfilled for me, O Allah make him my intercessor (*shaffihu fiyya*).

The *dua* contains the following steps:
1. Call and request to Allah stating that one uses the Prophet (ﷺ) as means.
2. Call to the Prophet (ﷺ) stating that one uses him as means to Allah.
3. Call and request to Allah to make the Prophet (ﷺ) one's intercessor.

This proves that:
• One may ask for the Prophet's intercession in this life.
• One takes for granted that the Prophet's intercession is accepted.
• One does not take for granted that one's own intercession is granted.
• Such intercession is "by means of him," period.

Albani says:

> And *shafaah* [the Arabic word used in the hadeeth] in the language means: *du'aa* [supplication], and this is what is meant for the *Shafaa'ah* which is established for him (SAW) and for the other prophets and the pious on the Day of Ressurection.[37]

The hadith is neither taking place on the Day of Resurrection, nor is it primarily about the Prophet's blessed

---

36 Albani, *Tawassul: Its Types and Rulings.*
37 *Ibid.*

shafaa, which is explained in countless other verses and hadith. Instead it is about *tawassul* through the Prophet (ﷺ), which is the method and language of asking for his *shafaa* here and now. Albani is attempting to make *tawassul* and *shafaa* one and the same thing. Furthermore, he is trying to make the language say something other than what it states explicitly:

> And this shows that *shafaah* is more particular than *du'aa* since it will only occur if there are two people seeking a matter, so that one of them is a supplicant for the other, as opposed to a single person seeking something who does not have anyone else to supplicate for him. In *Lisaan ul-Arab* it says, '*shafaa'ah* [intercession] is the intercessor's speaking to a king about a need which he is requesting for someone else, and the intercessor is the one seeking something for someone else, through whom he intercedes to attain what is desired...' So it is established by this means also that the *tawassul* of the blind man was through his (SAW) *du'aa* and not his person.[38]

Again, the hadith is about a request for intercession, and not the intercession itself. Clearly, a person hoping to have another intercede on his behalf must first ask the potential intercessor, out of respect for the intercessor's station.

Albani continues:

> That from what the Prophet (SAW) taught the blind man was, 'And accept my supplication [*shafaa'ah*] for him'... This sentence is an authentic part of the hadeeth, it is reported by Ahmad and al-Haakim who authenticated it with adh-Dhahabee agreeing. And it alone is a decisive proof that taking the hadeeth to refer to *tawassul* by his person is futile, that being the position of some recent writers - and it seems that they realise this point and therefore do not mention this sentence at all-which shows how far they can be trusted in reporting narrations. And close to this is their quoting the previous sentence, 'O Allaah accept his *shafaa'ah* for me', as a proof for

38. *Ibid*.

tawassul by his person - but as for explaining how it shows that then they do not explain that to the readers, since one not having something cannot give it to others.[39]

The proof for *tawassul* through the Prophet's person does not lie in the particular part of the *dua* which says "O Allah accept his *shafaa* for me," but in the *dua* as a whole, as demonstrated above.

Albani's contempt and mistrust of scholars whose views invalidate his are typical of his approach and that of his followers. It should be noted that he dismisses both Nawawi and Ibn al-Jawzi, who state that *tawassul* is through the Prophet's person and status, as "recent writers."

Albani says:

> 'I.e. accept my *shafaa'ah* for him, i.e. accept my *du'aa* that you accept his '*shafaa'ah*', i.e. his *du'aa* that You restore my sight.' And it is not possible to understand anything but this from this sentence [40]

This impossibility may seem clear to Albani, but to others it is clear that the statement quoted also refers to the phrase, "I ask you and turn to you by means of your Prophet (ﷺ)." Thus the full meaning is, "Accept my *dua* and accept the request that I may make this *dua* to you by means of him."

Albani argues:

> This is why you find the opponents feigning ignorance of it and not making mention of it since it demolishes their building from the foundations and tears down it's walls, and when they hear it you see them looking at you like one in a swoon. This is because they (think that they) understand the *shafaa'ah* of the Messenger (SAW) for the blind man, but what can the blind man's *shafaa'ah* for the Messenger (SAW) mean? They have no answer for that at all. And the fact that they percieve this nullifies their misinterpretation is that you will not find a

---

39 *Ibid.*
40 *Ibid.*

single one of them using it in practice, i.e. supplicating, 'O Allaah accept Your Prophet's *shafaa'ah* for me and my shafaa'ah for him.' [41]

The blind man was merely blind in the eyes, but Allah spoke of those who are blind-hearted and this is a more serious illness.

The *shafaa* of the Messenger for the blind man benefits the blind man, and the *shafaa* of the blind man for the Messenger benefits the blind man also! The first *shafaa* is the Prophet's request on behalf of the blind man, and the latter is the blind man's request that he be given permission to have the Prophet (ﷺ) request for him. It is very clear, but it seems Albani ekes out his contentions only in order to confuse the issue, just as he shuffled the lexical meanings of *tawassul* and *shafaa*.

> . . . the saying of the blind man in his *du'aa*, 'O Allaah I ask You and turn to You by means of your Prophet Muhammad (SAW)' means, 'I seek a means of nearness to You by means of the *du'aa* of your Prophet', with the governing word [i.e. *du'aa*] omitted - and this is something well known in the language - as occurs in the saying of Allaah, 'the town and caravan...' (12:82), i.e. 'the PEOPLE of the town, and the COMPANIONS of the caravan..' [with the governing words PEOPLE and CARAVAN omitted]. And we and the opponents agree upon that, i.e. that we have to come up with the governing word which has been omitted.[42]

The above is a good illustration of Albani's tendency to reduce the sense of the *dua*, which is, "I am turning to You by means of your Prophet (ﷺ)" to the more specific, "I am turning to You by means of your Prophet's *dua*." Albani utilizes terms that are not in the hadith, e.g. "by means of the *dua*," and he suggests that they are the terms that govern the meaning of the hadith.

Albani continues:

---

41 *Ibid.*
42 *Ibid.*

And in our view it is the same case as with the *du'aa* of Umar and his *tawassul* by means of al-Abbaas-either it is taken to be, 'I turn to You by means of the (status) of Your Prophet', and 'O Muhammad I turn by your (person) or your (position) to my Lord' - as they claim—or to be, 'I turn to you by means of the (*du'aa*) of Your Prophet', and, 'O Muhammad I turn to you by your (*du'aa*) to my Lord'—which is our saying. And one of these must be preferred due to a proof which shows it. So as for their saying that the missing governing word is (status/position) then they have no proof for it, neither in this or any other hadeeth, since there is nothing mentioned along with it which suggests or states any mention of (status) or indicates it at all.[43]

Here is perhaps the greatest fallacy in Albani's entire argument, since in asserting the above, he ignores the countless verses and hadiths that illustrate the Prophet's status. Among these are his own statements that he is the Master of the children of Adam, the noblest among them in Allah's sight, and firm in his praiseworthiness according to the *ijma* of Muslims.

Albani argues:

Just as they have nothing from the Quran and Sunnah, or from the practice of the Companions where there is *tawassul* by anyone's status. So this preferred view of theirs has nothing to support it and so is rendered baseless and not taken into any further consideration.

As for our view then it is supported by many proofs which have preceded.[44]

On the contrary, the lexical "proof" has been rejected, as *shafaa* is not the same as *tawassul*, and the "proof" that the *wasila* is simply the Prophet's *dua* has been rejected, as it was shown that the *wasila* is the Prophet (ﷺ) himself, in addition to the *dua* which he taught the blind man, and the *dua* which he himself made on his behalf.

Albani concludes:

43 *Ibid.*
44 *Ibid.*

And I also say, Even if it were correct that the blind man sought to make *tawassul* by his (SAW) person, then it would be something particular to him, not something shared by the rest of the prophets and the pious. And joining them in it along with him is something not acceptable, since he (SAW) was the leader and the most noble of them all, so it could have been something which Allaah particularised him like many others reported in authentic narrations, and matters of particularised qualities are not within the scope of analogy. So he who thinks that the blind man's *tawassul* to Allaah was by means of his (SAW) person-then he should halt at that and not add others to it, as is reported from Imaam Ahmad and Shaikh al-Izz bin abdis-Salaam (RH).[45]

One goes to one's nearest means among the *salihin*, or saintly people, as is established by Umar's *tawassul* through the Prophet's uncle, al-Abbas. This is not only permissible, but recommended by all recognized schools. As for Imam Ahmad, it has been reported that he made *tawassul* through the Prophet (ﷺ) a part of every *dua* and unlike Albani he never tried to alter the modality of the *tawassul* or its meaning.

In following Albani's somewhat contorted arguments it has been noted that he moved from denying that the *tawassul* can be made through the Prophet's person to accepting it, then denying that it may be made by anyone other than the blind man, then accepting it, and finally denying that it may be made through anyone other than the Prophet (ﷺ).

Despite Albani's recent innovations, it is abundantly clear that 1400 years of Islamic scholarship has shown that it is not forbidden to seek the Prophet's person as a means for obtaining remedies and blessings in this life, as the Companions and the Followers sought such blessings through the hair of the Prophet (ﷺ), his *minbar*, his sweat, his saliva, his grave, and other items. If one cannot deny the good obtained from a mere particle of the Prophet's body long after his time, then surely one cannot deny the good obtained from his noble person.

45 *Ibid.*

6. REFUTATION OF THOSE WHO QUESTION THE VALID ISLAMIC PRACTICE OF SEEKING BLESSINGS (*TABARRUK*) FROM THE PROPHET'S RELICS BY COMPANIONS WHO SOUGHT BLESSINGS FROM THE PROPHET'S PERSON AND RELICS

T*abarruk*: deriving blessing from something once owned or touched by a holy person. *Athar*: relics.

Allah Himself has recommended the *tabarruk* of His many prophets. For example, He mentioned the *tabarruk* of the Prophet Jacob (ﷺ) through the relic of his son Joseph (ﷺ), and the *tabarruk* of the Banu Israil through the relics of the Family of Moses (ﷺ) and of the Family of Aaron (ﷺ). The evidence for the *tabarruk* of the Companions and the *tabiin* through the Prophet (ﷺ) and the saints is immeasurable. Allah said:

> *Go with this my shirt, and cast it over the face of my father: he will come to see (clearly) . . . When the Caravan left (Egypt), their father said, I do indeed scent the presence of Yusuf . . . Then, when the bearer of glad tidings came, he laid it on his face and he became a seer once more. He said, Said I not unto you that I know from Allah that which ye know not?* (12:93-96).

And He said:

> *And their Prophet said unto them, Lo! the token of his kingdom is that there shall come unto you the ark wherein is peace of reassurance from your Lord, and a remnant of that which the house of Moses and the house of Aaron left behind, the angels bearing it. Lo! herein shall be a token for you if (in truth) ye are believers* (2:248).

6.1. THE PROPHET'S HAIR AND NAILS

There are countless hadith on this subject. For example, according to Bukhari:

Usman ibn Abd Allah ibn Mawhab said, "My family sent me to Umm Salama with a cup of water. Umm Salama brought out a silver bottle which contained one of the hairs of the Prophet (鷺), and it used to be that if anyone came under the evil eye or ill health they used to send her a cup of water through which she would pass this hair (for drinking). We used to look into the silver bottle; I saw some reddish hair."[1]

According to Bukhari, Anas said, "When the Prophet (鷺) shaved his head (after pilgrimage), Abu Talha was the first one to take of his hair."

According to Muslim, Anas also said, "The Prophet (鷺) threw stones at *al-jamra*, then sacrificed, then told the barber to shave his head right side first, then began to give the hair away to the people."

Anas said, "Talha was the one distributing it."[2]

According to Ahmad, he also said, "When the Prophet (鷺) shaved his head in Mina, he gave me the hair from the right side and he said: Anas! take it to Umm Sulaym [his mother]. When the Companions saw what the Prophet (鷺) gave us, they began to compete to take the hair from the left side, and everyone was taking a share from that."

Ibn al-Sakan narrated through Safwan ibn Hubayra from the latter's father: Thabit al-Bunani said, Anas ibn Malik said to me (on his death-bed), "This is a hair of Allah's Messenger, Allah's blessings and peace upon him. I want you to place it under my tongue." Thabit continued, I placed it under his

---

1 Bukhari, *Sahih*, in the Book of Clothing, under the chapter entitled, "What is mentioned about gray hair."
2 Muslim, Tirmidhi, Abu Dawud.

tongue, and he was buried with it under his tongue."[3]

Abu Bakr said, "I saw Khalid [ibn Walid] asking for the Prophet's forelock and he received it. He used to put it over his eyes and then kiss it." It is known that he then placed it in his *qalansuwa* (head cover around which the turban is tied) and never faced battle again except he won. Narrated by Ibn Hajar in his *Isaba*. Ibn Abi Zayd al-Qayrawani relates that Imam Malik said, "Khalid ibn al-Walid owned a *qalansiyya* (another linguistic form of *qalansuwa*) which contained some of the Prophet's hair, and that is the one he wore the day of the battle of Yarmuk.[4]

Ibn Sirin (one of the *tabiin*) said: "A hair of the Prophet (ﷺ) in my possession is more precious to me than silver and gold and everything that is on the earth and everything that is inside it." Bukhari, Bayhaqi (*Sunan kubra*), and Ahmad.

In *Sahih al-Bukhari*,[5] Uthman bin Abd Allah ibn Mawhab said, "My people sent me with a bowl of water to Umm Salama." Israil approximated three fingers indicating the small size of the container in which there was some hair of the Prophet (ﷺ). Uthman added, "If any person suffered from the evil eye or some other disease, he would send a vessel (containing water) to Umm Salama (and she would dip the Prophet's hair into it and it would be drunk). I looked into the container (that held the hair of the Prophet (ﷺ)) and saw a few reddish hair in it."

Hafiz Ibn Hajar said, "They used to call the silver bottle in which the hair of the Prophet (ﷺ) was kept *jiljalan* and that bottle was in the home of Umm Salama."[6]

Hafiz al-Ayni said:

> Umm Salama had some of the hair of the Prophet (ﷺ) in a silver bottle. When some people got ill, they would go and obtain blessings from these hairs and they would be healed by means of their blessings. If a person were struck by the evil eye or any sickness, he would send his wife to Umm Salama with a *mikhda-ba* or water-pail, and she would pass the hair through that water and then drink the water and he would be

---

3 Narrated by Ibn Hajar in *al-Isaba fi tamyiz al-sahaba* (Calcutta, 1983) 1:72 under "Anas ibn Mali."
4 Ibn Abi Zayd, *al-Jami fi al-sunan* (1982 ed.) p. 227.
5 *Sahih al-Bukhari*, Volum 7, Book 72, Number 784.
6 Ibn Hajar, *Fath al-bari*, Volume 10, pge 353.

healed, after which they would return the hair to the *jiljal*.[7]

Imam Ahmad narrates, from Abd Allah ibn Zayd ibn Abd Rabbih with a sound (*sahih*) chain, that the Prophet (ﷺ) clipped his nails and distributed them among the people.[8]

6.2. THE PROPHET'S SWEAT

Anas said: "The Prophet (ﷺ) stayed with us, and as he slept my mother began to collect his sweat in a flask. The Prophet (ﷺ) awoke and said, O Umm Sulaym, what are you doing? She said, This is your sweat which we place in our perfume and it is the best perfume." Muslim, Ahmad.

When Anas was on his deathbed he instructed that some of this flask be used on his body before his funeral and it was done. Bukhari. According to Ibn Sad, Ibn Sirin also was given some of Umm Sulaym's flask.

6.3. THE PROPHET'S SALIVA AND ABLUTION WATER

There are a great many hadiths that relate to *tabarruk* with the Prophet's saliva and ablution water.

In Bukhari and Muslim: The Companions would compete for whoever would get the remnant of the Prophet's ablution water in order to put it on their faces. Nawawi said, "In these narrations is evidence for seeking blessings with the relics of the saints" (*fihi al-tabarruk bi athar al-salihin*).[9]

The Prophet (ﷺ) used to heal the sick with his saliva mixed with some earth with the words, "*Bismillah*, the soil of our earth with the saliva of one or some of us shall heal our sick with our Lord's permission."[10]

Regarding this hadith, Ibn Hajar wrote:

> The Prophet's words "with the saliva of one or some of us" indicate that he would spit at the time of using a protective invocation (*ruqya*). Nawawi said (in *Sharh Sahih Muslim*), "The meaning of the hadith is that the Prophet (ﷺ) put some of his saliva on his

7 Hafiz al-Ayni, *Umdat al-qari*, Volume 18, page 79.
8 Imam Ahmad in his *Musnad* (4:42), according to Haythami in *Majma al-zawaid* (3:19).
9 Nawawi in *Sharh Sahih Muslim*.
10 Bukhari and Muslim.

forefinger then placed it on some earth and formed some clot with it with which he wiped the place of the ailment or the wound, pronouncing the words of the hadith at the time of wiping." Qurtubi said, "The hadith shows the permissibility of using protective invocations against any and all ailments, and it shows that this was an open and widely-known matter among them." He also said, "The Prophet's placing of his finger on the earth and of the earth on his finger indicates the desirability of doing this when using a protective invocation . . . This falls under none other than the heading of obtaining blessing (*tabarruk*) through Allah's Names and through what His Prophet ( ) left us." Ibn Hajar concludes, Protective invocations (*ruqa*) and those hanged upon oneself (*azaim*) have wondrous effects, the true nature of which boggles the mind.

According to all of Bukhari, Abu Dawud, Ahmad, and Bayhaqi, the Prophet ( ) would have everyone in Madina bring their newborn to him, whereupon he would read over them and do *nafth* and *tifl* (breath mixed with saliva) into their mouths. He would then instruct the mothers not to suckle them that day until nightfall. He did the same later in Makka. The names of over 100 of the Helpers (*ansar*) and Emigrants (*muhajirin*) who received this particular blessing have been transmitted with chains of transmission (*isnad*), and are found in the main books of biographies.

6.4. THE PROPHET'S CUP

Hajjaj ibn Hassan said, "We were at Anas' house and he brought up the Prophet's cup from a black pouch. He ordered that it be filled with water and we drank from it and poured some of it on our heads and faces and sent blessings on the Prophet ( ).[11] Asim said, "I saw that cup and I drank from it."[12]

6.5. THE PROPHET'S *MINBAR*

Ibn Umar used to touch the seat of the Prophet's *minbar* and then wipe his face for blessing.[13]

11 Ahmad, Ibn Kathir.
12 Bukhari.
13 *Al-Mughni* 3:559; *al-Shifa* 2:54; Ibn Sad, *Tabaqat* 1:13; *Mawsuat fiqh Abdullah ibn Umar* p. 52

From Abu Hurayra, Jabir, Abu Imama, and Malik: The Prophet (ﷺ) made it a *sunna* to swear to the truth from his *minbar*.[14] Ibn Hajar says, and in Makka, one swears between the Yemeni corner and the Station of Abraham (*maqam ibrahim*).[15]

6.6. MONEY THE PROPHET (ﷺ) GAVE AWAY

Jabir sold a camel to the Prophet (ﷺ) and the latter gave instructions to Bilal to add a *qirat* (1/12 dirham) to the agreed sale price. Jabir said, "The Prophet's addition shall never leave me," and he kept it with him after that.[16]

6.7. THE PROPHET'S STAFFS

When Abdullah ibn Anis came back from one of the battles having killed Khalid ibn Sufyan ibn Nabih, the Prophet (ﷺ) gifted him his staff and said to him, "It will be a sign between you and me on the Day of Resurrection." Thereafter he never parted with it and it was buried with him when he died.[17]

Qadi Iyad relates that after Jihjah al-Ghifari took the Prophet's staff from the hands of Uthman and tried to break it across his knee, infection seized his knee which led to its amputation, and he died before the end of the year.[18]

6.8. THE PROPHET'S SHIRT

Jabir says, "The Prophet (ﷺ) came after Abdullah ibn Ubay had been placed in his grave. He ordered that he be brought out. He placed his hands on Abdullah's knees, breathed (*nafth*) upon him mixing it with saliva, and dressed him with his shirt.[19]

---

14 Nisai, Ahmad, Abu Dawud, Ibn Majah, and others. Bukhari confirms it.
15 Ibn Hajar, *Fath al-bari.*
16 Bukhari.
17 Narrated by Ahmad in his *Musnad* (3:496).
18 Qadi Iyad in his book *al-Shifa* in the chapter entitled, "Esteem for the things and places connected with the Prophet.
19 Bukhari and Muslim.

6.9. THE PROPHET'S PLACES OF PRAYER (*MUSALLA*)

Many chains of transmission: Utban ibn Malik was one of the Companions of the battle of Badr. After he became blind he said to the Prophet (🕌), "I would like you to pray in my house so that I can pray where you prayed." The Prophet (🕌) went to his house and asked where exactly he would like him to pray. He indicated a spot to him and the Prophet (🕌) prayed there. The version in Muslim has, I (Utban) sent for the Prophet (🕌) the message, "Come and lay for me a place for worship (*khutt li masjidan*)."[20] Imam Nawawi said, "It means, "Mark for me a spot that I can take as a place for worship by obtaining blessing from your having been there (*mutabarrikan bi atharika*) . . . In this hadith is evidence for obtaining blessings through the relics of saints (*al-tabarruk bi athar al-salihin*)."[21]

Umar feared that the taking of the tree of the *baya* to the Prophet (🕌) as a place of prayer might lead to a return to idol-worship and he had it cut.[22] It is known, however, that Ibn Umar derived blessings even from walking in the same spots where the Prophet (🕌) had walked and praying exactly where he had prayed both at the Kabah and on his travels, and that he watered a certain tree under which Prophet (🕌) had prayed so that it would not die.[23]

6.10. THE PROPHET'S GRAVE

Dawud ibn Salih says: "[The Caliph] Marwan [ibn al-Hakam] one day saw a man placing his face on top of the grave of the Prophet (🕌). He said, "Do you know what you are doing?" When he came near him, he realized it was Abu Ayyub al-Ansari. The latter said, "Yes; I came to the Prophet (🕌), not to a stone."[24]

Muadh ibn Jabal and Bilal also came to the grave of the

20 Bukhari and Muslim.
21 Imam Nawawi, *Sharh sahih Muslim*.
22 Bukhari, Ibn Sad (1:73).
23 Bukhari, Bayhaqi (*Sunan* 5:245).
24 Ibn Hibban in his *Sahih*, Ahmad (5:422), Tabarani in his *Mujam al-kabir* (4:189) and his *Awsat* according to Haythami in *al-Zawaid* (5:245), al-Hakim in his *Mustadrak* (4:515); both the latter and al-Dhahabi said it was *sahih*. It is also cited by al-Subki in *Shifa al-siqam* (p. 126), Ibn Taymiyya in *al-Muntaqa* (2:261f.), and Haythami in *al-Zawaid* (4:2).

Prophet (ﷺ) and sat weeping, and the latter rubbed his face against it. [25]

Hafiz al-Dhahabi writes in the compendium of his shaykhs:

> Ahmad ibn al-Munim related to us . . . [with his chain of transmission] from Ibn Umar that the latter disliked to touch the Prophet's grave. I say, He disliked it because he considered it disrespect. Ahmad ibn Hanbal was asked about touching the Prophet's grave and kissing it and he saw nothing wrong with it. His son Abd Allah related this from him.[26]

Dhahabi continues,

> If it is said, "Why did the Companions not do this?" It is replied, "Because they saw him with their very eyes when he was alive, enjoyed his presence directly, kissed his very hand, nearly fought each other over the remnants of his ablution water, shared his purified hair on the day of the greater Pilgrimage, and even if he spat it would virtually not fall except in someone's hand so that he could pass it over his face. Since we have not had the tremendous fortune of sharing in this, we throw ourselves on his grave as a mark of commitment, reverence, and acceptance, even to kiss it. Don't you see what Thabit al-Bunani did when he kissed the hand of Anas ibn Malik and placed it on his face saying, "This is the hand that touched the hand of Allah's Messenger"? Muslims are not moved to these matters except by their excessive love for the Prophet (ﷺ), as they are ordered to love Allah and the Prophet (ﷺ) more than they love their own lives, their children, all human beings, their property, and paradise and its maidens. There are even some believers that love Abu Bakr and Umar more than themselves . . .
>
> Don't you see that the Companions, in the excess of their love for the Prophet (ﷺ), asked him, "Should we not prostrate to you?" and he replied no, and if he had allowed them, they would have prostrated to him as a mark of utter veneration and respect, not as a

---

25 Ibn Majah 2:1320, Ahmad, Tabarani, Subki, and Ibn Asakir.

26 Al-Dhahabi, *Mujam al-shuyukh* (1:73) in the entry devoted to his shaykh Ahmad ibn Abd al-Munim al-Qazwini (#58).

mark of worship, just as the Prophet (ﷺ) Joseph's brothers prostrated to Joseph (ﷺ). Similarly the prostration of the Muslim to the grave of the Prophet (ﷺ) is for the intention of magnification and reverence. One is not imputed disbelief because of it whatsoever (*la yukaffaru aslan*), but he is being disobedient [to the Prophet's injunction to the Companions]. Let him therefore be informed that this is forbidden. Similarly in the case of one who prays towards the grave.

Imam Ahmad's son Abd Allah said, I asked my father about the man who touches and kisses the pommel of the Prophet's minbar to obtain blessing, or touches the grave of the Prophet (ﷺ). He responded by saying, "There is nothing wrong with it." Abd Allah also asked Imam Ahmad about the man who touches the Prophet's *minbar* and kisses it for blessing, and who does the same with the grave, or something to that effect, intending thereby to draw closer to Allah. He replied, "There is nothing wrong with it."[27]

As already mentioned, there is an authentic account that, in the time of Umar, there was a drought during which Bilal ibn Harith came to the grave and said, "O Messenger of Allah, ask Allah for rain on behalf of your Community."

Also as already mentioned, there is Aisha's account whereby she instructed that the roof be opened over the Prophet's grave in times of drought, and it would rain.

Umar sent a message to Aisha saying, "Will you allow me to be buried with my two companions (the Prophet (ﷺ) and Abu Bakr)?" She said, "Yes, by Allah," though it was her habit that if a man from among the Companions asked her that she would always refuse.[28]

6.11. THE PROPHET'S ROBE OR CLOAK (*JUBBA*)

Imam Muslim relates that Abd Allah, the freed slave of Asma, the daughter of Abu Bakr, the maternal uncle of the son of Ata, said, "Asma sent me to

27 This was narrated by Abdullah ibn Ahmad ibn Hanbal in his book entitled al-*Ilal fi marifat al-rijal* (2:492).
28 Bukhari.

Abdullah ibn Umar saying, 'The news has reached me that you prohibit the use of three things: the striped robe, saddle cloth made of red silk, and fasting the whole month of Rajab. 'Abd Allah said to me, 'So far as what you say about fasting in the month of Rajab, how about one who observes continuous fasting? And so far as what you say about the striped garment, I heard Umar ibn al-Khattab say that he had heard from Allah's Messenger, "He who wears a silk garment, has no share for him (in the Hereafter)." And I am afraid that stripes were part of it. And so far as the red saddle cloth is concerned, here is Abd Allah's saddle cloth [= his] and it is red.' I went back to Asma and informed her, so she said, 'Here is the cloak (*jubba*) of Allah's Messenger,' and she brought out to me that cloak made of Persian cloth with a hem of (silk) brocade, and its sleeves bordered with (silk) brocade, and said, 'This was Allah's Messenger's cloak with Aisha until she died, then I got possession of it. The Apostle of Allah used to wear it, and we washed it for the sick so that they could seek cure thereby.' Muslim relates this in the first chapter of the book of clothing. Nawawi comments: "In this hadith is a proof that it is recommended to seek blessings through the relics of the righteous and their clothes (*wa fi hadha al-hadith dalil ala istihbab al-tabarruk bi aathaar al-salihin wa thiyabihim*)."[29]

6.12. OBJECTS, LOCATIONS AND PEOPLE THE PROPHET (ﷺ) TOUCHED

Suwayd ibn Ghafalah reported: I saw Umar kissing the Black Stone and clinging to it, saying, "I saw Allah's Messenger bearing great love for you." This hadith has been narrated on the authority of Sufyan with the same chain of transmitters (and the words are), "He (Umar) said, "I know that you are a stone, nor would I consider you of any worth, except that I saw Abu al-Qasim bearing great love for you." And he did not mention about clinging to it.[30]

Qadi Iyad relates that Imam Malik would not ride an animal in Madina and he used to say, "I am too shy before Allah to trample with an animal's hoof on the earth where Allah's

---

29 *Sharh Sahih Muslim* (Book 37 Chapter 2 #10).
30 Muslim: 7:2916.

Messenger is buried."³¹ Imam Malik gave a *fatwa* that whoever said, "The soil of Madina is bad" be given thirty lashes and jailed. Qadi Iyad mentions the verses of an anonymous visitor to Madina:

The veil is lifted from us and a moon shines out
    to those who look on, banishing all illusions.
When our mounts reach Muhammad, it is forbidden
    for us to be found in our saddles.
We are drawing near to the best man ever
    to walk on the earth,
So we hold this ground in respect and honor.

Iyad adds, "One must respect the places . . . whose soil contains the body of the Master of Mankind and from which the *din* of Allah and the *sunna* of the Messenger spread out . . . and the first earth that the skin of the Prophet (ﷺ) touched after death. Its fragrance should be inhaled and its residences and walls should be kissed." Then he recites:

O Abode of the best of the Messengers . . .
For you (Madina) I have intense love, passionate love,
    and yearning which kindles the embers of my heart.
I have a vow: If I fill my eyes with those walls
    and the places where you (O Prophet) walked,
There my turbaned gray hair will be covered with dust
    from so much kissing.
Had it not been from obstacles and foes,
I would always visit them,
    even if I had to be dragged by my feet.³²

Al-Tabarani and Imam Ahmad narrated through Handhalah Ibn Hudhaym that the latter went with his grandfather, Hudhaym, to the Prophet (ﷺ). Hudhaym said to the Messenger of Allah, "I have sons and grandsons, some of whom are pubescent and others still children." Motioning to the young child next to him, he said, "This is the youngest." The Prophet (ﷺ) brought this young child whose name was Handhalah next to him, wiped on his head, and told him,

31 Qadi Iyad, *Shifa*, in the chapter entitled "Esteem for the things and places connected with the Prophet."
32 Trans. Aisha Bewley in *Muhammad the Messenger of Allah: ash-Shifa of Qadi Iyad* p. 248.

"barakallahu fik," which means, "May Allah bless you." After that, people started to bring Handhalah a person with a swollen face or a sheep with a swollen udder. Handhalah would place his hand on that part of his head the Prophet (ﷺ) wiped, then touch the swollen part and say *bismillah*, and the swelling would be cured.[33]

Ibn Abi Shayba narrated: Yazid ibn Abd al-Malik ibn Qusayt and al-Utbi narrated that it was the practice of the Companions in the masjid of the Prophet (ﷺ) to place their hands on the pommel of the hand rail (*rummana*) of the pulpit (*minbar*) where the Prophet (ﷺ) used to place his hand. There they would face the *qibla* and supplicate to Allah hoping He would answer their supplication because they were placing their hands where the Prophet (ﷺ) placed his while making their supplication. Abu Mawduda said, "And I saw Yazid ibn Abd al-Malik do the same."

This practice of the Companions clarifies two matters. The first is the permissibility of asking Allah for things by the Prophet (ﷺ) (*tawassul*) after his death since by their act the Companions were truly making *tawassul*. Likewise it is permissible to ask Allah for things by other pious Muslims. The second is the permissibility of seeking blessings (*baraka*) from the objects the Prophet (ﷺ) touched.[34]

The *tabii* Thabit al-Bunani said he used to go to Anas Ibn Malik, kiss his hands, and say, "These are hands that touched the Prophet (ﷺ)." He would kiss his eyes and say, "These are eyes that saw the Prophet (ﷺ)."[35]

According to Bukhari, Abd al-Rahman ibn Razin related that one of the Companions, Salama ibn al-Aku, raised his hands before a group of people and said, "With these very hands I pledged allegiance (*baya*) to the Messenger of Allah," upon hearing which, all who were present got up and went to

---

33 Al-Tabarani, *al-Awsat* and *al-Kabir* (4:16); Imam Ahmad, *Musnad* (5:67-68) with a sound chain as stated by al-Haythami in *al-Zawaid* (4:211).

34 Related by Ibn Abi Shayba, *Musannaf* (4:121), in the chapter entitled, "Touching the grave of the Prophet" with a sahih chain according to Ibn Hajar al-Asqalani and Qadi Iyad in his book a*l-Shifa* in the chapter entitled, "Concerning the visit to the Prophet's grave, the excellence of those who visit it and how he should be greeted."

35 Abu Yala narrated it in his *Musnad* (6:211) and Ibn Hajar mentions it in his *al-Matalib al-aliya* (4:111). Al-Haythami declared it sound in *Majma al-zawaid* (9:325).

kiss his hand. Another version of this hadith was also related by Ahmad.[36]

Abu Malik al-Ashjai said that he once asked another Companion of the Tree, Ibn Abi Awfa, "Give me the hand that swore *baya* to the Messenger of Allah, blessings and peace upon him, that I may kiss it." Ibn al-Muqri related it.

Bukhari also relates that Suhayb saw Sayyidina Ali kiss both the hand and feet of the Prophet's uncle al-Abbas, and that Thabit kissed the hand of Anas because it had touched the Prophet's hand.[37]

Al-Shurunbali al-Hanafi, in his manual of *Fiqh* entitled *Nur al-idah*, said:

> It is praiseworthy to enter into the Holy House [Kabah]. The person who enters it should seek the place where the Prophet (ﷺ) performed his ritual prayer. This place is in front of him when his back faces the door, so that there is the distance of three cubits between him and the door in front of him. He will perform ritual prayer in it. If he performs it near the wall, he will put his cheek on it, and pray to Allah for forgiveness and praise Him.[38]

6.13. THE SOIL AND VEGETATION OF MADINA

The merits of Madina, of prayer in Madina, of visiting the Masjid al-Nabawi, of living in Madina, of not cutting its trees, etc. are all based on the fact that the Prophet (ﷺ) is there. The fact that it is a sanctuary (*haram*) and a preserve (*hima*) is well documented in hadith. It is even strongly recommended not to enter Madina except on foot, and many Companions, *tabiin*, and *tabi al-tabiin*, never entered it except on foot, out of respect for the Holy Presence of the Prophet (ﷺ).

Ali ibn Abu Talib narrated:

> The Prophet (ﷺ) said, "Madina's fresh grass is not to be cut, its game is not to be driven away, and things dropped in it are to be picked up only by one who publicly announces it, and it is not permissible

36 Bukhari in his *Adab al-mufrad*.

37 *Ibid*.

38 Al-Hanafi in the book of pilgrimage of his manual of *fiqh* entitled *Nur al-idah* (as translated by Muhammad Abul Qasem under the title *Salvation of the Soul and Islamic Devotions*) said (p. 225).

for any man to carry weapons in it for fighting, and it is not advisable that its trees are cut except what a man cuts for the fodder of his camel.[39]

Abu Hurayra narrated:

When the people saw the first fruit (of the season or of plantation) they brought it to Allah's Apostle. When he received it he said, "O Allah, bless us in our fruits; and bless us in our city; and bless us in our *sa*'s and bless us in our *mudd* (i.e. in every measure). O Allah, Ibrahim was Thy servant, Thy friend, and Thy apostle; and I am Thy servant and Thy apostle. He (Ibrahim) made supplication to Thee for (the showering of blessings upon) Makka, and I am making supplication to Thee for Madina just as he made supplication to Thee for Makka, and the like of it in addition." He would then call to him the youngest child and give him these fruits. [40]

As the Prophet (ﷺ) asked Allah's blessings on the entire city and its fruits, then Madina must be full of blessing, as his supplication is a *dua mustajab*, or answered prayer. Therefore, it is common practice for pilgrims to purchase dates from Madina for the blessings, and to bring them back home to share among those who could not make the pilgrimage. It is said that there remain living some of the date palms planted by the holy hand of the Most Noble Messenger himself, blessings and peace be upon him.

6.14. HIS HAND AND HIS FEET

The first hadith Imam Ahmad related from Anas ibn Malik in his *Musnad Anas* is, "The whole Community of the people of Madina used to take the hand of the Prophet (ﷺ) and rush to obtain their need with it."[41]

Aisha, the Mother of the Believers, narrated: "The Messenger of Allah, may Allah bless him and grant him peace, when he had a complaint, would recite the last three *surah*s of Quran, over himself and blow." She said, "When his pain was great, I would recite it over him and wipe him with his right hand hoping for its blessing."[42]

39 Abu Dawud, 10:2030.
40 Muslim, 7:3170.
41 Ahmad, *Musnad* 3:98 (#11947).
42 Narrated by Malik in *al-Muwatta*, Book 50, Number 50, 4:10.

Usama ibn Sharik narrates:

I went to see the Prophet (ﷺ) while his Companions were with him, and they seemed as still as if birds had alighted on top of their heads. I gave him my salam and I sat down. [Then Bedouins came and asked questions which the Prophet (ﷺ) answered.] . . . The Prophet (ﷺ) then stood up and the people stood up. They began to kiss his hand, whereupon I took his hand and placed it on my face. I found it more fragrant than musk and cooler than sweet water.[43]

Abd Allah ibn Umar narrated:

Ibn Umar was sent with a detachment by the Apostle of Allah. The people wheeled round in flight. He said, "I was one of those who wheeled round in flight. When we stopped, we said, 'What should we do? We have run away from the battlefield and deserve Allah's wrath.' Then we said, 'Let us enter Madina, stay there, and go there while no one sees us.' So we entered the city and thought, 'If we present ourselves before Allah's Apostle, and if there is a chance of repentance for us, we shall stay; if there is something else, we shall go away.' So we sat down (waiting) for the Apostle of Allah before the dawn prayer. When he came out, we stood up to him and said, 'We are the ones who have fled.' He turned to us and said, 'No, you are the ones who return to fight after wheeling away.' We then approached and kissed his hand, and he said, 'I am the main body of the Muslims.'"[44]

Ibn Umar told a story and said, "We then came near the Prophet (ﷺ) and kissed his hand." It is related in Ibn Majah's

---

43 Narrated by Abu Dawud (#3855), Tirmidhi (2038—*hasan sahih*), Ibn Majah (3436), al-Hakim (4:399), and Ahmad (4:278). *Al-hafiz* Imam Bayhaqi cites it in Branch 15 of his *Shuab al-iman* entitled: The Fifteenth Branch of Faith, Namely A Chapter on Rendering Honor to the Prophet, Declaring His High Rank, and Revering Him (*al-Khamis ashar min shuab al-iman wa huwa babun fi atazim al-nabi sallallahu alayhi wa sallama wa ijlalihi wa tawqirih*) Vol. 2 p. 200 (#1528).

44 Abu Dawud, Book 14 [*Jihad*], Number 2641. This hadith is also found in *al-Abhari*; in the book of *al-hafiz* Ibn Muqri on standing up and kissing the hand out of respect; in the *Adab al-mufrad* of Imam Bukhari (Chapter on Kissing the Hand and Chapter on Kissing the Foot), in Ibn Majah (*Adab*) in Bayhaqi's *Dalail an-nubuwwa*, and in the *Musnad* of Ahmad ibn Hanbal.

Sunan, in Abu Dawud's *Sunan*, and in the *Musannaf* of Ibn Abi Shayba through two different chains.[45]

Umm Aban, daughter of al-Wazi ibn Zari narrated that her grandfather Zari al-Abdi, who was a member of the deputation of Abd al-Qays, said, "When we came to Madina, we raced to be first to dismount and kiss the hand and foot of Allah's Apostle . . . (to the end of the hadith)."[46]

Bukhari relates from her a similar hadith in his *Adab al-mufrad*: We were walking and someone said, "There is the Messenger of Allah," so we took his hands and feet and kissed them.

Burayda narrated that one of the Bedouin Arabs who came to the Prophet (ﷺ) asked, "O Messenger of Allah, give me permission to kiss your head and your hands," and he received it. In another version, he asks permission to kiss the head and the feet.[47]

Safwan ibn Asal al-Muradi reports: "One of two Jews said to his companion, 'Take us to this Prophet (ﷺ) so we can ask him about Musa's ten signs'. . . [the Prophet (ﷺ) replied in full and then] they kissed his hands and feet and said, 'we witness that you are a Prophet (ﷺ) . . .'"[48]

Qadi Iyad and al-Bazzar narrate:

> When we were with Allah's Messenger on an expedition, a Bedouin came and asked for a miracle. The Prophet (ﷺ) pointed at a tree and said to the Bedouin, "Tell that tree, Allah's Messenger summons you." The tree swayed and brought itself out, and came to the presence of the Prophet (ﷺ) saying, "Peace be upon you O Messenger of Allah!" The Bedouin said, "Now let it return to its place!" When Allah's Messenger ordered it, the tree went back. The Bedouin said, "let me prostrate to you!" The Messenger answered, "No one is allowed to do that [i.e. it is *haram*]." The

---

45 Ibn Majah, Book of *Adab*, Chapter on kissing by a man of another man's hand; and Abu Dawud, Book of *Adab*, Chapter on kissing the hand.

46 Abu Dawud, 41:5206.

47 Narrated in Ghazali's *Ihya* and the version mentioning the feet is in Hakim's *Mustadrak* and in Ibn Muqri. Both al-Hakim and al-Iraqi declared the latter's chain authentic.

48 Narrated by Ibn Abi Shayba (Book of *Adab*, Chapter entitled A Man Kissing Another Man's Hand When He Greets Him), Tirmidhi (Book of *Adab*) who declared it *hasan sahih*, al-Nisai, Ibn Majah (Book of *Adab*), and al-Hakim who declared it *sahih*.

Bedouin said, "Then I will kiss your hands and feet."
The Prophet (ﷺ) permitted him that.[49]

6.15. THE PROPHET'S BLESSED SKIN
Usayd ibn Hudayr narrated:

> Abd al-Rahman ibn Abi Layla, quoting Usayd ibn
> Hudayr, a man of the Ansar, said that while he was
> given to jesting and was talking to the people and
> making them laugh, the Prophet (ﷺ) poked him
> under the ribs with a stick. He said, Let me take
> retaliation. He said, Take retaliation. He said, You are
> wearing a shirt but I am not. The Prophet (ﷺ) then
> raised his shirt and the man embraced him and began
> to kiss his side. Then he said, This is what I wanted,
> Apostle of Allah![50]

Ibn Abd al-Barr relates that the Prophet (ﷺ), after forbidding two or three times the use of *khaluq* (a kind of perfume mixed with saffron), and finding that Sawad ibn Amr al-Qari al-Ansari was wearing it, nudged him in the mid-section with a palm-tree stalk (*jarida*) and scratched him. The latter asked for reparation, and when the Prophet (ﷺ) bared his own belly to him, he jumped and kissed the Prophet's belly.[51]

Ibn Ishaq's version in the *Sira* mentions that Sawad was standing in the ranks of the Companions of Badr at the time of this incident. The Prophet (ﷺ) was arranging the ranks with his switch (*miqraa*) and he nudged Sawad's belly with it, scratching him inadvertently, and said, "Align yourself with the others." Sawad said, "Ya Rasulallah, you hurt me, so give me reparation." The Prophet (ﷺ) handed him the switch and said, "Take reparation." Sawad approached him and kissed his belly. The Prophet (ﷺ) said, "What made you do that, O Sawad?" He replied, "Ya Rasulallah, the time has come for what you see, and I loved for my last action in this *dunya* to be touching you."

Buhaysa al-Fazariyya narrated: "My father sought permission from the Prophet (ﷺ). Then he came near him, lifted his

---

49 Narrated by Qadi Iyad in *al-Shifa* (1:299) and al-Bazzar in his *Musnad* (3:49).
50 Abu Dawud, Book 41, Number 5205.
51 Ibn Abd al-Barr, *Istiab fi marifat al-ashab* (p. 673).

shirt, and began to kiss him and embrace him out of love for him."[52]

6.16. PLACES THE PROPHET (ﷺ) VISITED
Abu Burda narrated:

> When I came to Madina, I met Abdullah bin Salam. He said, "Will you come to me so that I may serve you with *sawiq* (i.e. powdered barley) and dates, and let you enter a (blessed) house in which the Prophet (ﷺ) entered?. . ."[53]

6.17. HIS FOOD
Bukhari narrates:

> The Messenger (ﷺ) lived in Abu Ayyub's house until his mosque and dwelling-houses were built; then he moved to his own quarters. Yazid ibn Abu Habib from Marthad ibn Abd Allah al-Yazani from Abu Ruhm al-Samai told me that Abu Ayyub told him, "When the Messenger (ﷺ) came to lodge with me in my house he occupied the ground floor, while I and Umm Ayyub were above. I said to him, "O Prophet of Allah, you are as dear to me as my parents, and I am distressed that I should be above and you below me. So leave your present quarters and exchange places with us." He replied, "O Abu Ayyub, it is more convenient for me and my guests that we should be on the ground floor of the house." So we remained as we were. Once we broke a jar of water and Umm Ayyub and I took one of our garments to mop up the water in fear that it would drop on the Prophet (ﷺ) and cause him annoyance. We had no cloth which we could use. We used to prepare his evening meal and send it to him. When he returned what was left, Umm Ayyub and I used to touch the spot where his hand had rested and eat from that in the hope of gaining a blessing.

6.18. HIS ARROWS
Ibn Hisham narrates:

---

52 Abu Dawud, Book 9, Number 1665.
53 Bukhari, Volume 5, Book 58, Number 159.

The Apostle ordered the force to turn to the right through the salty growth on the road which leads by the pass of al-Murar to the declivity of al-Hudaybiyya below Makka. They did so, and when the Quraysh cavalry saw from the dust of the army that they had turned aside from their path they returned at a gallop to Quraysh. The Apostle went as far as the pass of al-Murar and when his camel knelt and the men said, "The camel won't get up," he said, "It has not refused and such is not its nature, but the One who restrained the elephant from Makka is keeping it back. Today whatever condition Quraysh make in which they ask me to show kindness to kindred I shall agree to." Then he told the people to dismount. They objected that there was no water there by which they could halt, so he took an arrow from his quiver and gave it to one of his companions and he took it down into one of the waterholes and prodded the middle of it and the water rose until the men's camels were satisfied with drinking and lay down there.[54]

6.19. THE PROPHET'S SANDALS

Bukhari and Tirmidhi narrate from Qatada: "I asked Anas to describe the sandals of Allah's Messenger and he replied, 'Each sandal had two straps,'" and from Isa ibn Tahman: "Anas took out a pair of shoes and showed them to us. They did not have hair on them."[55]

Bukhari, Malik, and Abu Dawud relate that Ubayd ibn Jarih said to Abd Allah ibn Umar, "I saw you wear tanned sandals." He replied, "I saw the Prophet (ﷺ) wearing sandals with no hair on them and perform ablution in them, and so I like to wear them."

Al-Qastallani said that Ibn Masud was one of the Prophet's servants and that he used to bring for the Prophet (ﷺ) his cushion (wisada), his tooth-stick (siwak), his two sandals (nalayn), and the water for his ablution. When the Prophet (ﷺ) rose he would put his sandals on him; when he sat he would carry his sandals in his arms until he rose.[56]

---

54 Ibn Hisham, *Sirat rasul Allah*, translated by A. Guillaume as "The Life of Muhammad" p. 500-501.

55 The remark refers to the Arabian practice of not removing the hair from the leather from which shoes were made.

56 Al-Qastallani, *al-Mawahib al-laduniyya* (Beirut, 1996 ed.) 1:429.

Qastallani mentions the following from one of the greatest *tabiin*:

> Abu Ishaq (al-Zuhri) said, al-Qasim ibn Muhammad (ibn Abu Bakr al-Siddiq) said, Of the proven blessing of the likeness of the Prophet's sandal is that whoever has it in his possession for *tabarruk*, it will safeguard him from the sedition of rebels and the mastery of enemies, and will be a barrier against every recreant devil and the evil eye of the envious. If the pregnant woman holds it in her right hand at the time of labor, her delivery will be easier by Allah's change and His might.

Al-Qastallani also said that Abu al-Yaman ibn Asakir wrote a volume on the image of the Prophet's sandal, as did Ibn al-Hajj al-Andalusi. He relates the account of a pious shaykh by the name of Abu Jafar Ahmad ibn Abd al-Majid:

> I cut the pattern of this sandal for one of my students. He came to me one day and said, "I saw a wonder yesterday from the blessing of this sandal. My wife was suffering from a pain which almost took her life. I placed the sandal on the spot of her pain and said, 'O Allah, show me the blessing of the owner of this sandal.' Allah cured her on the spot."[57]

Al-Munawi and al-Qari mention that Ibn al-Arabi said that the sandals are part of the attire of prophets, and the people only left them due to the mud in their lands.[58] He also mentioned that one of the names of the Prophet (ﷺ) in the ancient books is *sahib al-nalayn* or "The wearer of the two sandals."

Shaykh Yusuf al-Nabahani recited about the Prophet's sandals:

> *wa nalun khadana haybatan li waqariha*
> *fa inna mata nakhdau li haybatiha nalu*
> *fa daha ala ala al-mafariqi innaha*
> *haqiqataha tajun wa surataha nalu*
> A sandal to whose majestic nobility we submit
> For by submitting to its majesty do we rise:

---

57 *Ibid.* 2:174.
58 Al-Munawi and al-Qari in their commentaries on Tirmidhi's *al-Shamail*.

Therefore place it in the highest spot for it is
In reality a crown, though its image is a sandal.

When Imam al-Fakhani first saw the Prophet's sandals he recited:

wa law qila li al-majnuni layla wa wasluha
turidu am al-dunya wa ma fi zawayaha
laqala ghubarun min turabi nialiha
ahabbu ila nafsi wa ashfa li balawaha
And if Layla's Madman were asked: do you prefer
Union with Layla, or the world and its treasures

He would answer: "Dust from the earth of her sandals is dearer to my soul, and its most soothing remedy."

Both Shihab al-Din Ahmad al-Muqri and Ashraf Ali al-Tahanawi, the Deobandi shaykh, wrote whole works on the Prophet's sandals.[59]

The *muhaddith* of India Muhammad Zakariyya Kandhalwi said in his translation of Tirmidhi's *Shamail*:

> Maulana Ashraf Ali Thanwi Sahib has written in his book *Zaadus Saeed* a detailed treatise on the *barakat* and virtues of the shoes of *Rasulullah Sallallahu Alayhi Wasallam*. Those interested in this should read that book (which is available in English). In short, it may be said that it [the Prophet's sandal] has countless qualities. The *ulama* have experienced it many a time. One is blessed by seeing *Rasulullah Sallallahu Alayhi Wasallam* in one's dreams; one gains safety from oppressors and every heartfelt desire is attained. Every object is fulfilled by its *tawassul* (means, petition, request). The method of *tawassul* is also mentioned therein.[60]

6.20. HIS WAIST-WRAP

Malik narrates:

---

59 Al-Muqri's book is named *Fath al-mutaal fi madh al-nial* (The opening of the Most High in the praise of the Prophet's sandals), and Ashraf Ali al-Tahanawi's treatise is entitled *Nayl al-shifa bi naal al-mustafa* (Obtaining remedy through the sandals of the Elect One) found in his book *Zad al-said* (Provision for the fortunate). Both are quoted in al-Sayyid Hashim al-Rifai's *Adilla* p. 101.

60 Maulana Muhammad Zakariyya Kandhalwi, ed. and trans. of Tirmidhi, *al-Shamail al-muhammadiyya*, 2nd ed. (Ghaziabad, India: New Era Publishers, 1994) pl 72-73.

Yahya related to me from Malik from Ayyub ibn Abi Tamima as-Sakhtyani from Muhammad ibn Sirin that Umm Atiyya al-Ansariyya said: The Messenger of Allah, may Allah bless him and grant him peace, came to us when his daughter died and said, "Wash her three times, or five, or more than that if you think it necessary, with water and lotus leaves, and at the end put on camphor, or a little camphor, and when you have finished let me know." When we finished we told him, and he gave us his waist-wrapper and said, "Shroud her with this."[61]

From all of the above evidence it is seen that *tawassul* and *tabarruk* are an intimate and integral part of the practice of the Companions, that both are *sunna*, and that none of the mainstream Islamic scholars deny it.

---

61 Malik, *Muwatta*, Book 16, Number 16.1.2.

GLOSSARY

ahkam: legal rulings.

ahl al-bida wa al-ahwa: the People of Unwarranted Innovations and Idle Desires.

ahl al-sunna wa al-jamaa: the Sunnis; the People of the Way of the Prophet and the Congregation of Muslims.[1]

*aqid*a pl. *aqad*: doctrine.

azaim: strict applications of the law. These are the modes of conduct signifying scrupulous determination to please one's Lord according to the model of the Prophet (ﷺ).

bida: blameworthy innovation.

faqih, pl. *fuqaha*: scholar of *fiqh* or jurisprudence; generally, "person of knowledge."

faqir, pl. *fuqara*: Sufi, lit. "poor one."

fatwa, pl. *fatawa*: legal opinion.

fiqh: jurisprudence.

fitna: dissension, confusion.

hadith: saying(s) of the Prophet, and the sciences thereof.

hafiz: hadith master, the highest rank of scholarship in hadith.

haqiqi: literal.

hashwiyya: uneducated anthropomorphists.

hijri: adjective from *hijra* applying to dates in the Muslim calendar.

hukm, pl. *ahkam*: legal ruling.

ibadat: worship, acts of worship.

ihsan: perfection of belief and practice.

ijtihad: personal effort of qualified legal reasoning.

isnad: chain of transmission in a hadith or report.

istinbat: derivation (of legal rulings).

jahmi: a follower of Jahm ibn Safwan (d. 128), who said: "Allah is the wind and everything else."[2]

jihad: struggle against disbelief by hand, tongue, and heart.

kalam: theology.

khalaf: "Followers," general name for all Muslims who lived after the first three centuries.

khawarij: "Outsiders," a sect who considered all Muslims who did not follow them, disbelievers. The Prophet said about them as related by Bukhari: "They will transfer the Quranic verses meant to refer to disbelievers and make them refer to believers." Ibn Abidin applied the name of khawarij to the Wahhabi movement.[3]

madhhab, pl. *madhahib*: a legal method or school of law in Islam. The major schools of law include the Hanafi, Maliki, Shafii, and Hanbali and Jafari.

majazi: figurative.

manhaj, minhaj: Way, or doctrinal and juridical method.

muamalat (pl.): plural name embracing all affairs between human beings as opposed to acts of worship *(ibadat)*.

muattila: those who commit *tatil*, i.e. divesting Allah of His attrib-

---

1 See the section entitled "Apostasies and Heresies" in our *Doctrine of Ahl al-Sunna Versus the "Salafi" Movement* p. 60-64.

2 See Bukhari, *Khalq afal al-ibad*, first chapter; Ibn Hajar, *Fath al-bari, Tawhid*, first chapter; and al-Baghdadi, *al-Farq bayn al-firaq*, chapter on the Jahmiyya.

3 al-Sayyid Muhammad Amin Ibn Abidin al-Hanafi, *Radd al-muhtar ala al-durr al-mukhtar, Kitab al-Iman, Bab al-bughat* [Answer to the Perplexed: A Commentary on "The Chosen Pearl," Book of Belief, Chapter on Rebels] (Cairo: Dar al-Tibaa al-Misriyya, 1272/1856) 3:309.

utes.

muhaddith: hadith scholar.

muhkamat: texts conveying firm and unequivocal meaning.

mujahid, pl. *mujahidin*: one who wages *jihad*.

mujassima (pl.): those who commit *tajsim*, attributing a body to Allah.

mujtahid: one who practices *ijtihad* or personal effort of qualified legal reasoning.

munafiq: a dissimulator of his disbelief.

mushabbiha (pl.): those who commit *tashbih*, likening Allah to creation.

mushrik, pl. *mushrikun*: one who associate partners to Allah.

mutakallim, pl. *mutakallimun*: expert in *kalam*.

mutashabihat (pl.): texts which admit of some uncertainty with regard to their interpretation.

mutazila: rationalist heresy of the third century.

sahih: sound (applied to the chain of transmission of a hadith).

salaf: the Predecessors, i.e. Muslims of the first three centuries.

salafi: what pertains to the "Salafi" movement, a modern heresy that rejects the principles of mainstream Islam

shafaa: intercession.

sharia: name embracing the principles and application of Islamic law.

suluk: rule of conduct, personal ethics.

tawil: figurative interpretation.

tafwid: committing the meaning to Allah.

tajsim: attributing a body to Allah

tajwid: Quran reading.

takyif: attributing modality to Allah's attributes.

tamthil: giving an example for Allah.

taqlid: following qualified legal reasoning.

tariqa: path, specifically the Sufi path.

tasawwuf: collective name for the schools and sciences of purification of the self.

tashbih: likening Allah to His Creation.

tatil: divesting Allah from His attributes.

tawassul: seeking a means.

tawhid: Islamic doctrine of monotheism.

tazkiyat al-nafs: purification of the self.

usul: principles.

wasila: means.

BIBLIOGRAPHY

Abbas, Abul, and Abul Qasim al-Azafi, *Kitab al-durr al-munazzam.*
Abidin, Ibn, *Hashiyat al-durr al-mukhtar.*
Abidin, Ibn, *Radd al-muhtar* (Kuitah, Pakistan ed.).
Adi, Ibn, *al-Kamil fi al-duafa.*
Ahmad, *Kitab al-zuhd.*
Ahmad, *Musnad.*
Albani, *Daif al-adab al-mufrad.*
Albani, *Silsilat al-ahadith al-sahiha.*
Amruni, Abd al-Hayy al- and Abd al-Karim Murad, *Hawla kitab al-hiwar ma al-Maliki.*
Ansari, Al-Harawi al-, *Ilal al-maqamat.*
Ansari, Al-Harawi al-, *Manazil al-sairin*, Station 96.
Arabi, Ibn al-, *Aridat al-ahwadhi.*
Arabi, Muhammad Nawawi ibn Umar ibn, *Fath al-samad al-alim ala Mawlid al-Shaykh ibn al-Qasim / al-Bulugh al-fawzi li-bayan alfaz Mawlid Ibn al-Jawzi* (Cairo: Tubia bi nafaqat Fada Muhammad al-Kashmiri al-Kutubi, 1328/1910).
Asakir, Ibn , *Tarikh Dimashq.*
Asakir, Ibn, *Mukhtasar tarikh Dimashq.*
Asakir, Ibn, *Tanzih al-Sharia.*
Asbahani, Al-hafiz Abu Nuaym al-, *al-Targhib.*
Asbahani, Al-hafiz Abu Nuaym al-, *Hilyat al-awliya.*
Askari, al-, *al-Amthal.*
Asqalani, Ibn Hajar al-, *al-Durar al-kamina fi ayn al-miat al-thamina.*
Asqalani, Ibn Hajar al-, *al-Matalib al-aliya* (Kuwait, 1393/1973).
Asqalani, Ibn Hajar al-, *Fath al-bari sharh sahih al-Bukhari.*
Asram, Ibn, *Kitab al-istiqama.*
Athir, Ibn al-, *Usud al-ghaba.*
Azafi, Abul Abbas al- and Abul Qasim al-Azafi, *Kitab ad-durr al-munazzam.* (unpublished).
Azraqi, Al-, *Akhbar Makka.*
Baghawi, *Sharh al-sunna.*
Baghdadi, *al-Farq bayn al-firaq.*
Battuta, Ibn, *Rihla.*
Baydawi, *Anwar al-tanzil* in *Majma al-tafasir.*
Bayhaqi, al-, *Hayat al-anbiya fi quburihim.*
Bayhaqi, *Dalail al-nubuwwa.*
Bayhaqi, *Hayat al-anbiya* and *Shuab al-iman.*
Bayhaqi, *Manaqib al-Shafii.*
Bayhaqi, *Shuab al-iman.*
Bayhaqi, *Sunan al-kubra.*
Bazzar, al-, *Musnad.*
Bewley, Aisha Bint Abdurrahman, trans. *Muhammad Messenger of Allah: ash-Shifa of Qadi Iyad*, 2nd ed. (Granada: Madinah Press, 1992).
Biqai, al-, *Unwan al-zaman.*
Bukhari, *Adab al-mufrad.* 1990 Abd al-Baqi Beirut edition.
Bukhari, *Khalq afal al-ibad.*
Bukhari, *Sahih.*
Dahlan, Ahmad ibn Zayni, *al-Sira al-nabawiyya wa al-athar al-muhammadiyya.*
Daraqutni, *Sunan.*
Darimi, *Musnad.*

Dawud, Abu, *Sunan.*
Daylami, *al-Firdaws.*
Dhahabi, *Mujam al-shuyukh.*
Dhahabi, *Siyar alam al-nubala,* ed. Shuayb Arnaut (Beirut: Muassasat al-Risalah, 1981).
Dimashqi, Hafiz Shamsuddin Muhammad ibn Nasir al-Din al-, *Mawrid al-sadi fi mawlid al-hadi.*
Diyarbakri, al-, *Tarikh al-Khamis.*
Dunya, Ibn Abi al-, *Kitab al-ikhwan.*
Fasi, al-, *Shifa al-gharam.*
Ghazali, *al-Munqidh min al-dalal,* Damascus 1956.
Ghazali, *Ihya ulum al-din.*
Guillaume, A. trans., *The Life of Muhammad: A Translation of Ishaqs Sirat Rasul Allah.*
Habib, Sadi Abu, *Mawsuat al-ijma fi al-fiqh al-islami.*
Hajar, Ibn, *al-Isaba fi tamyiz al-Sahaba.*
Hajar, Ibn, *Fath al-bari* (Beirut: Dar al-kutub al-ilmiyya, 1410/1989).
Hajj, Ibn al-, *Kitab al-madkhal.*
Hakim, *Marifat ulum al-hadith.*
Hakim, *Mustadrak.*
Hanafi, al-Sayyid Muhammad Amin Ibn Abidin al-, *Radd al-muhtar ala al-durr al-mukhtar, Kitab al-Iman, Bab al-bughat.* (Cairo: Dar al-Tibaa al-Misriyya, 1272/1856).
Hanafi, Al-Tahanawi al-, *Kashshaf istilahat al-funun* (Beirut, 1966).
Hanafi, Al-Turkumani al-, *Kitab al-luma fi al-hawadith wa al-bida* (Stuttgart, 1986).
Hanafi, Ibn Zahira al-, *al-Jami al-latif fi fasl Makka wa ahliha.*
Hanbali, Al-hafiz Ibn Rajab al-, *Jami al-uloom wa al-hikam.*
Hanifa, Abu, *al-Fiqh al-akbar.*
Hasani, Shaykh Muhammad ibn Alawi al-Maliki al-, *Mafahim yajib an tusahhah.* Dubai: Hashr ibn Ahmad Dalmook, 4th ed. 1407/1986.
Hawwa, Said, *al-Sira bi lughati al-shir wa al-hubb.*
Haytami, *al-Jawhar al-munazzam.*
Haytami, Ibn Hajar al-, *Fatawa hadithiyya* (Cairo: Halabi, 1390/1970).
Haytami, Ibn Hajar al-, *Kitab al-mawlid al-sharif al-muazzam.*
Haytami, Ibn Hajar al-, *Mawlid al-nabi* (Damascus, 1900).
Haythami, Ibn Hajar al-, *al-Jawhar al-munazzam.*
Haythami, Ibn Hajar al-, *Majma al-zawaid.*
Hibban, Ibn, *Sahih.*
Hisham, Ibn, *Sira* (Beirut, dar al-wifaq ed.).
Hisham, Ibn, *Sirat rasul Allah.* trans. A. Guillaume. 9th printing (Karachi: Oxford U. Press, 1990).
Humayri, Shaykh Issa ibn Abd Allah ibn Mani al-, *Al-ilam bi istihbab shadd al-rihal li ziyarati qabr khayr al-anam alayhi al-salat was-salam.*
Iyad, Qadi, *al-Shifa fi marifat huquq al-mustafa,* ed. al-Bajawi.
Jamaa, Ibn, *Hidayat al-salik.*
Jawzi, Abu al-Faraj Ibn al-, *Mawlid al-arus* (Cairo, 1850).
Jawzi, Ibn al-, *al-Wafa.*
Jawzi, Ibn al-, *Mawlid al-arus.* (Damascus: maktabat al-hadara, 1955).
Jawzi, Ibn al-, *Muthir al-azm al-sakin ila ashraf al-amakin.*
Jawzi, Ibn al-, *Muthir al-gharam al-sakin ila ashraf al-amakin* (Cairo: Dar al-hadith, 1415/1995).
Jawzi, Ibn al-, *Sifat al-safwa* (Beirut: Dar al-kutub al-ilmiyya, 1409/1989).
Jaziri, Abd al-Rahman al-, *al-Fiqh ala al-madhahib al-arbaa.*

Jilani, *al-Ghunya*, ed. Farj Tawfiq al-Walid (Baghdad: Maktabat al-sharq al-jadida, n.d.).

Jilani, Abd al-Qadir al-, *Futuh al-ghayb*.

Jubayr, Ibn, *Kitab al-rihal*.

Jubayr, Ibn, *Ribal*.

Jurjani, Al-Sharif al-, *Kitab al-tarifat*.

Kathir, Ibn, *al-Bidaya wa al-nihaya* (Beirut and Riyad: Maktabat al-maarif & Maktabat al-Nasr, 1966).

Kathir, Ibn, *Mawlid al-nabi*.

Kathir, Ibn, *Mawlid rasulillah sallallahu alayhi wa sallam*. Salah al-Din al-Munajjad (Beirut: Dar al-Kitab al-Jadid, 1961).

Kathir, Ibn, *Sirat al-nabi*.

Kathir, Ibn, *Tafsir*.

Khatib, Abu al-Abbas Ahmad ibn al-, *Wasilat al-islam bi al-nabi alayhi al-salat wa al-salam*. (Beirut: Dar al-gharb al-islami, 1404/1984).

Khuzayma, Ibn, *Sahih*.

Lucknawi, Abu al-Hasanat al-, *Zafr al-amani sharh mukhtasar al-sayyid al-sharif al-Jurjani fi mustalah al-hadith* edited by Abd al-Fattah Abu Ghudda (Aleppo and Beirut: Maktab al-matbuat al-islamiyya, 3rd ed. 1416).

Majah, Ibn, *Iqamat al-salat wa al-sunnat*.

Majah, Ibn, *Sunan*.

Malik, *Kitab al-ruh*.

Maliki, Al-hafiz al-Turtushi al-, *Kitab al-hawadith wa al-bida*.

Maliki, Ibn al-Hajj al-Abdari al-, *Madkhal al-shar al-sharif* (Cairo, 1336 H).

Maliki, Shaykh Muhammad ibn Alawi al-, *al-Bayan wa al-tarif fi dhikra al-mawlid al-sharif*.

Maliki, Shaykh Muhammad ibn Alawi al-, *Mafahim yajib an tusahhah*.

Maliki, Shaykh Muhammad ibn Alawi al-, *Shifa al-fuad bi ziyarati khayr al-ibad*.

Mindah, Ibn, *Marifat al-sahaba*.

Misri, al-, *The Reliance of the Traveller*, trans. Nuh Ha Mim Keller.

Mubarak, Ibn al-, *Kitab al-zuhd*.

Mundhiri, *al-Targhib wa al-tarhib*.

Mundhiri, *Talkhis al-habir*.

Muslim, *Sahih*.

Nabahani, *Jami karamat al-awliya*.

Nahrawali, al-, *al-Ilam bi-alam bayt Allah al-haram*.

Najjar, Ibn al-, *Akhbar al-Madina*.

Najjar, Ibn al-, *al-Durra al-thamina fi akhbar al-madina*.

Naqqash, al-, *Shifa al-gharam*.

Nasafi, *Madarik al-tanzil*.

Nasai, *Amal al-yawm wa al-laylat*.

Nawawi, *Adhkar*. 1970 Riyadh edition.

Nawawi, *Adhkar*. 1988 Taif edition.

Nawawi, *Adhkar*. 1992 Mecca edition.

Nawawi, *al-Idah fi manasik al-hajj* (Damascus: *dar ibn Khaldun*, n.d.)

Nawawi, al-Majmu.

Nawawi, *al-Rawda*.

Nawawi, *al-Taqrib wa al-taysir*.

Nawawi, *al-Tarkhis fi al-ikram bi al-qiyam li dhawi al-fadl wa al- maziyya min ahl al-islam ala jihat al-birr wa al-tawqir wa al-ihtiram la ala jihat al-riya wa al-izam*. ed. Kilani Muhammad Khalifa (Beirut: Dar al-Bashair al-islamiyya, 1409/1988).

Nawawi, *Idah fi Manasik al-hajj*.

Nawawi, *Kitab al-Adhkar* (Beirut: al-Thaqafiyya).

Nawawi, *Kitab al-Adhkar*, ed. Abd al-Qadir al-Arnaut. *Dar al-Huda, Riyadh*, 1409/1989.
Nawawi, *Sharh sahih Muslim* (Khalil al-Mays ed., Beirut: Dar al-Qalam).
Nawawi, *Tahdhib al-asma wa al-lughat* (Cairo: Idarat al-Tibaah al-Muniriyah, 1927), Nisaburi, Abu Sad al-, *Sharaf al-mustafa*
Nisai, *Sunan.*
Nuaym, Abu, *Akhbar asbahan.*
Nuaym, Abu, *al-Targhib.*
Nuaym, Abu, *al-Tibb al-nabawi.*
Nuaym, Abu, *Hilyat al-awliya.*
Nuaym, Abu, *Marifat al-sahaba.*
Qari, Ali al-, *al-Asrar al-marfua.*
Qari, Ali al-, *Jam al-wasail fi sharh al-shamail.*
Qari, Ali al-, *Sharh al-shifa* (Beirut: Dar al-kutub al-ilmiyya ed. 2:149).
Qastallani, al-, *al-Mawahib al-laduniyya bi al-minah al-muhammadiyya.*
Qayyim, Ibn al-, *Kitab al-ruh.*
Qayyim, Ibn, *Madarij al-salikin.*
Qudama, Ibn, *al-Riqqa.*
Qunfudh, Ibn, *Wasilat al-islam bi al-nabi alayhi al-salat wa al-salam* (Beirut: Dar al-gharb al-islami, 1404/1984).
Qushayri, *Risala* (Cairo, 1319 ed.).
Razi, Tammam al-, *al-Fawaid.*
Rifai, al-Sayyid Hashim al-, *Adilla Ahl al-sunna wa al-jamaa.*
Sad, Ibn, *Tabaqat.*
Sakhawi, Shams al-Din al-, *al-Jawahir wa al-durar fi tarjamat shaykh al-islam Ibn Hajar.*
Sakhawi, Shams al-Din al-, *al-Qawl al-badi fi al-salat ala al-habib al-shafi* (Beirut 1987/1407).
Sakhawi, Shams al-Din al-, *Maqasid al-hasana.*
Sakhawi, *Tarjimat shaykh al-islam qutb al-awliya Abi Zakariyya al-Nawawi.*
Samhudi, *Khulasat al-wafa.*
Samhudi, *Saadat al-darayn.*
Samhudi, *Wafa al-wafa.*
Saqqaf, Shaykh Hassan ibn -Ali al-,*al-Ighatha bi adillat al-istighatha*, (Maktabat al-Imam Nawawi, Amman 1410/1990).
Shakir, Ahmad Muhammad, *Riyadh*. (1949 edition).
Shama, Al-hafiz Abu, *al-Baith ala inkar al-bida wa al-hawadith,* ed. Mashhur Hasan Salman (Riyadh: Dar al-Raya, 1990/1410). Cairo edition.
Sharani, *al-Tabaqat al-kubra* (1343/1925).
Sharawi, Imam Mutawalli, *Maidat al-fikr al-islamiyya.*
Shatibi, al-, *Kitab al-itisam* (Beirut ed.).
Shawkani, *al-Badr at-tali.*
Shawkani, *Nayl al-awtar*, Dar al-kutub al-ilmiyya.
Shawkani, *Tuhfat al-dhakirin*. 1970 Beirut: Dar al-kutub al-ilmiyya.
Shayba, Ibn Abi, *Musannaf.*
Shaykh, Abu al-, *Kitab al-salat alu ul-nabi.*
Siraj, al-, *al-Luma.*
Subki, *Shifa al-siqam.*
Suyuti, *al-Khabar al-dall ala wujud al-qutb wa al-awtad wa al-nujaba wa al-Abdal.*
Suyuti, *al-Khasais al-kubra.*
Suyuti, *al-Laali al-masnua.*
Suyuti, *Anba al-adhkiya bi hayat al-anbiya.*
Suyuti, *Hawi li al-fatawi.*

Suyuti, *Husn al-maqsid fi amal al-mawlid* in *al-Hawi li al-fatawi.*
Suyuti, *Jami al-saghir.*
Suyuti, *Manahil al-safa fi takhrij ahadith al-shifa* (Beirut 1988/1408).
Suyuti, *Tabyid al-sahifa.*
Suyuti, *Tadhkirat al-mawduat.*
Suyuti, *Tafsir al-durr al-manthur*
Tabarani, *al-Awsat.*
Tabarani, *al-Mujam al-kabir.*
Tabari, Ibn Jarir al-, *Tafsir.*
Taftazani, al-, *Madkhal ila al-tasawwuf.*
Tahanawi, *Inja al-watan.*
Tahawi, *Mushkil al-athar.*
Taymiyya, Ibn, *al-Aqida al-wasitiyya* (Cairo: al-matbaa al-salafiyya, 1346).
Taymiyya, Ibn, *al-Furqan bayna awliya al-shaytan wa awliya al-rahman,* 2nd ed. (Beirut: al-maktab al-islami, 1390/1970).
Taymiyya, Ibn, *al-Ziyara.*
Taymiyya, Ibn, *Fatawa.*
Taymiyya, Ibn, *Iqtida al-sirat al-mustaqim.*
Taymiyya, Ibn, *Majma fatawa Ibn Taymiyya.* King Khalid ibn Abd al-Aziz edition.
Taymiyya, Ibn, *Majmua al-fatawa al-kubra* (1398 ed.).
Taymiyya, Ibn, *Mukhtasar al-fatawa al-misriyya* (al-Madani Publishing House, 1400/1980).
Taymiyya, Ibn. *Dar taarud al-aql wa al-naql,* ed. Muhammad al-Sayyid Julaynid (Cairo: Muassasat al-ahram, 1409/1988).
Tirmidhi, Shaykh al-Hakim al-, *Adab al-muridin.*
Tirmidhi, Shaykh al-Hakim al-,*Aridat al-ahwadhi.*
Uwayda, Salah Muhammad ed., Nawawis *al-Taqrib wa al-taysir* (Beirut: dar al-kutub al-ilmiyya, 1407/1987).
Wahhab, Muhammad Ibn Abd al-, *al-Usul al-thalatha.*
Wahhab, Muhammad ibn Abd al-, *Three Principles of Oneness.*
Wansharisi, Al-, *al-Mustahsan min al-bida.*
Yala, Abu, *Musnad* (Dar al-Mamun ed. 1407/1987).
Zabidi, al-, *Ithaf al-sada al-muttaqin.*
Zahawi, Al-, *The Doctrine of Ahl al-Sunna,* trans. Sh. Hisham Kabbani (Mountain View: ASFA, 1996).

INDEX TO QURANIC VERSES

INDEX TO HADITH

More people than the collective tribes of Banu Tamim, 7

My Community shall not agree on an error, 84

My Community, my Community, 26

My family sent me to Umm Salama, 136

My father sought permission from the Prophet, 151

My intercession is for those people of my Community who commit major sins, 26, 31

My life is a great good for you, 55, 121

No one is allowed to do that, 150

No people sit at length without mentioning Allah, 100

No you are the ones who return to fight after wheeling away, 149

None of them dies except Allah substitutes another in his place, 62-63

O Allah, bless us in our fruits, 148

O Allah, grant forgiveness to my mother, 78

O Allah, Lord of Gabriel, 78

O Allah, Thou art its Lord, 29

O Commander of the believers, 46, 62

O Messenger of Allah, ask Allah for rain, 124, 143

O Messenger of Allah, he said it in dissimulation, 85

O my Lord, I spare no effort except in what escapes my power, 54, 123-124

O People! Remember Allah, 98

O so-and-so son of so-and-so, 83

O Umm Sulaym, what are you doing, 138

On the gate of paradise is written, 43

One is raised in the company of those he loves, 11

One of two Jews said to his companion, 150

One will be told: Stand, O so-and-so, 30

Pray as you see me pray, 112

Recite, 53, 57, 74, 88, 120, 148

Send much blessings upon me, 95

Take retaliation, 151

Take this to Abu Ubayda, 124

Talha was the one distributing it, 136

The actions of human beings are shown to me, 121

The actions of human beings are shown to me every Thursday, 121

The best of your days is Friday, 98

The earth will never lack forty men similar to Abraham, 63

The earth will never lack forty men similar to the Friend of the Merciful, 63

The first people who came to us, 107

The night I was enraptured and taken up to heaven, 42

The night I was enraptured I saw a green garment on the Throne, 43

The one who leaves his house for prayer, 77

The people suffered a drought, 54, 124

The Prophet came after Abdullah ibn Ubay had been placed in his grave, 140

The Prophet threw stones at al-

GENERAL INDEX

ENCYCLOPEDIA OF ISLAMIC LAW SERIES